MUSIC RIGHTS

WITHOUT FIGHTS

The Smart Marketer's Guide To
Buying Music For Brand Campaigns

Richard Kirstein

 PRESS

First published in Great Britain 2015

by Rethink Press (www.rethinkpress.com)

© 2015 Richard Kirstein

PRAISE

"This book shines a light on the dark art of music licensing and is essential reading for client-side Marketing and Procurement music buyers who want to know the right questions to ask."
Steve Lightfoot, Senior Manager – Global Marketing Procurement,
World Federation of Advertisers

"Music rights can be impenetrably complex for marketers. This book really simplifies how rights work and how to license them with better control of cost and risk."
Paul Hibbs – Head of Brand and Advertising, Nationwide Building Society

"Richard has been a pioneer in the development of new ways to procure music that gives brands more options and an ability to gain access to great music at reasonable cost. If you regularly develop video and are often looking for music, this book will help you better navigate this complex world."
Dominic Chambers – Global Head of Digital Marketing, Jaguar Land Rover

"The right music can be a blessing or a curse for brand builders. *Music Rights Without Fights* tips the scales for marketers with easy-to-follow steps to engage the music industry for mutual benefit."
Billy Burgess – Senior Global Communications Manager,
Absolut – The Absolut Company – Pernod Ricard

CONTENTS

To Jenni and Ivor, for the best start on the journey.

To Joe and Zac, in the hope they go further than I do.

FOREWORD

There is little doubt that the right choice of music can transform a piece of content or TV ad from being good to being truly memorable. Music can have incredible emotional power and can really build brand equity power and appeal. The music business has been through a traumatic period of declining revenues as recorded music revenues evaporate, and so the income from music syncs has become an ever greater part of their remaining profitability. It is therefore essential that you are well informed and have access to the right professional advice to obtain the right music at the right price, otherwise brands will continue to pay over the odds for music rights.

Richard has been a pioneer in the development of new ways to procure music that gives brands more options and an ability to gain access to great music at reasonable cost. If you regularly develop video and are often looking for music this book will help you better navigate this complex world.

Dominic Chambers
Global Head of Digital Marketing, Jaguar Land Rover

INTRODUCTION

All brands know that music is a powerful passion point; so great music in commercials and online videos can significantly increase consumer engagement which helps to drive sales. However, finding the right track is only the start; the real challenge occurs when brands try to license music and navigate the fragmented music rights industry.

I've written *Music Rights Without Fights* to empower brand marketers by explaining how the music rights industry really works. Using my insider knowledge, brand marketers can fully embrace this practical step-by-step guide to cost and risk management and license the music they want, with less pain.

During my career spanning more than twenty years in the music licensing business, I've developed a unique insight acting for both music rights owners and buyers. This perspective allows me to clearly articulate the cultural gap between the music industry on the one side and the brand world on the other. It's a relationship often fraught with misunderstanding and sometimes a lack of mutual respect. This can create a cycle of unilateral deal making in which brands feel less than satisfied.

It's been my mission to educate brands on music rights and how best to license them. I've worked with some of the world's largest consumer brands, particularly in the fashion, automotive, financial services and alcoholic beverage sectors; explaining the role of all the parties involved and the tactics to drive convergent agendas for better commercial outcomes. I've gained a maverick reputation for (i) teaching brands the tips the music industry would rather they didn't know and (ii) for collaborating with marketing procurement specialists and trade bodies who champion the benefits of de-coupling TV production from creative agencies, which of course includes music.

Music Rights Without Fights explains the framework I've developed for brands to strike smarter music deals from a stronger bargaining position. As a consultant, I'm often engaged as "fire fighter" when deals have gone wrong. I frequently see the same problems, many of which can be avoided with the right knowledge and tactics.

This book contains a step-by-step guide to cost drivers and tools to manage them. These are rooted in competitive tendering i.e. the practice that treats music sourcing as an opportunity for music rights owners within a competitive environment. I debunk some of the common urban myths and stress the importance of bringing music much earlier into the planning process.

Brands sometimes fail to fully respect that music is intellectual property ("IP") controlled by third parties who will fiercely protect it from unlicensed use. We'll examine how unauthorised usage occurs and how to avoid it by aligning media schedules with licence terms.

Why now? The trend towards decoupled TV production has been growing in strength since the late 2000s with some markets further ahead than others. In the UK, the industry trade bodies, Incorporated Society Of British Advertisers ("ISBA") and Chartered Institute of Procurement & Supply ("CIPS"), have helped educate their members whilst internationally the World Federation of Advertisers ("WFA") has been very influential. I've had the privilege to speak to the members of all three organisations and delegates at the ProcureCon conference. In these sessions I encountered a keen appetite to learn more about music rights procurement with a view to decoupling it from creative agencies.

Now is therefore an appropriate moment to publish the first practical guide to music rights, licensing and procurement specifically written for brands. It comes at a time when several pioneering UK brands have already fully decoupled TV production from their creative agencies, moving it into international production agencies. My consultancy, Resilient Music, has been fortunate to collaborate with these companies who are focused on process and efficiency without undue influence on the creative musical direction from their clients' creative agencies.

Music Rights Without Fights has been written specifically for brand marketers and their colleagues in marketing procurement who want to understand how music rights work and engage with the music industry in a less adversarial manner. I hope you find it useful.

SECTION ONE
How is the music industry structured?

In this section, we'll unpick the key components of the fragmented music rights industry. Primarily, the difference between songs and recordings; their respective owners, music publishers and record labels. We'll then examine the role of performers; both featured and non-featured artists, and their respective representatives.

So the take-out for marketers is this:

- **The record label controlling a cover version will usually be different from the record label that controls the original artist recording (unless both artists happen to be signed to the same label).**
- **The music publisher controlling the underlying song remains constant irrespective of the recording.**
- **You must license both song and recording to use the music you want**

Re-records

Having looked at covers, let's now consider re-records which are another version of an existing song. This is a frequently misunderstood term, so let's get a few points clear from the start:

"Re-record", as commonly understood within the advertising and marketing sectors, means a newly commissioned sound recording of an existing song. Usually it is specifically created for use in a marketing campaign and does *not* contain any elements of the original artist recording. That said, sometimes recording artists will re-record their earlier songs once they're free from restrictions of a record label recording contract.

"Re-mix" usually means taking digital audio file "stems", which may have been copied from the original multi-track recording session tape, to create a new mix specifically for use in a marketing campaign. It *does* contain elements of the original artist recording.

"Re-working", "Re-invention", "Re-imagining". These terms have no commonly understood meaning among music rights owners, brands and agencies so their use may potentially encourage copyright infringement even when innocently used by marketers and agency teams.

Why do brands and agencies use re-records?

- **Re-records are usually, though not always, cheaper for a brand or agency to license than the original artist master recording.**
- **Re-records allow the opportunity to present a well-known song in a different guise.**

In the UK, the retailer John Lewis has won both industry and consumer praise for their Christmas TV campaigns which usually feature famous songs covered in an engaging way. Examples include:

Guns N' Roses' "Sweet Child O Mine" – covered by Taken By Trees
Elton John's "Your Song" – covered by Ellie Goulding
The Smiths' "Please Let Me Get What I Want" – covered by Slow Moving Millie
Keane's "Somewhere Only We Know" – covered by Lily Allen

Now let's consider where re-records are sourced from. Broadly speaking, re-records are created by two different supplier groups:

- **Professional arrangers / producers, who may be part of a music production company. Typically they are not exclusively signed to a record label.**
- **Recording artists who typically are exclusively signed to a record label.**

The approach required to successfully navigate the above supplier groups varies significantly but can be summarised as follows:

Professional arrangers / producers

- **Engagement / Commissioning Agreement**
- **One contracting party – arranger / producer or music production company**
- **Should include all sub-contractors e.g. session musicians, studios**
- **Re-record can be agreed on a licence or assignment basis**
- **Song must still be licensed separately and additionally from the applicable music publisher(s)**

Recording artist

- **Artist's recording services agreement – via artist's manager**
- **Artist waiver – via artist's record label**
- **Master synchronisation licence – via artist's record label**
- **Agreed on a licence basis only**
- **Artist's record label will own the recording even though brand financed it**
- **Song must still be licensed separately and additionally from applicable music publisher(s)**

(iii) The urban myths around Public Domain

The topic of "public domain" or "out of copyright" is usually misunderstood by brands and agencies which can lead to very expensive mistakes when incorrect assumptions are made. My explanation here is designed to be practical for marketers rather than drafted in legal language. Across most European Union (EU) States, the current copyright laws dictate that:

- **Songs, compositions and lyrics are in copyright until seventy years after the end of the year in which the creator died. Where there are multiple creators, the entire work remains in copyright until seventy years after the end of the year in which the last creator died.**
- **Sound recordings are in copyright until seventy years after the end of the year in which they were first commercially released.**

On the surface this seems simple and so many marketers and agencies mistakenly assume they can start using songs or sound recordings which they believe to be out of copyright without paying licence fees. Sadly, that assumption is flawed for several reasons:

Generally

Whilst there is almost a harmonisation of copyright law across members of the European Union, laws vary elsewhere, especially in the USA. Therefore, for any online marketing campaign that isn't geo-locked to specific markets, there's significant risk that a song or recording that is out of copyright in one market might still be in copyright elsewhere.

Songs / Compositions

In the UK, it's perfectly legal to register a new arrangement of an out of copyright song or composition as a new work. For example, if a brand or agency commissions a music production company to create a new arrangement of "Eine Kleine Nacht Muzik" by Wolfgang Amadeus Mozart (1756-1791), they will almost certainly register their new arrangement as a new work and charge a license fee for its use. The key proviso is that the supplier must use Mozart's original score as a reference and not copy another registered arrangement.

Following this idea, even if a brand wishes to use an existing recording of an out of copyright song or composition, it's often the case that someone has already registered the arrangement as a new work. Even if it's a recording of a classical composer's original manuscript score, sometimes the conductor or ensemble leader will register their interpretation as a new arrangement – so the new work is in copyright.

Smart brands keep a watchful eye on compositions that "fall out of copyright". For example, in 2005 the classical works of Edward Elgar and Gustav Holst became public domain in Europe given that both composers died in 1934. I recall hearing Elgar's famous "Nimrod" from *Enigma Variations* in UK radio commercials in early 2005 where brands or agencies took advantage of the work's change in status. The same would be true for Holst's *The Planets* of which "Mars, The Bringer Of War" is well known.

Most recently, a ruling by a US federal judge has deemed the copyright claim to "Happy Birthday" to be invalid in the USA which may be of comfort to American producers of video content. That said, the work remains in copyright in other markets so the situation is far from simple for brands wishing to use it in a global context.

Sound recordings
There's a perspective among some music lawyers that a new copyright exists in a newly mastered version of an out of copyright sound recording. To clarify, this argument

accepts that nothing has changed to the sound recording other than an upgrade in the sonic quality usually by digital audio processing to remove hiss, crackle and other noises. Across most EU States, any sound recording that was commercially released more than seventy years ago should theoretically be public domain. However, that assumption would only be truly safe if you could access an original 78 rpm shellac gramophone record dating from that era rather than a re-mastered vinyl disc, CD or digital audio file from a later time period. To support the argument that the sound recording is public domain, you need an actual physical copy that's more than seventy years old.

Also, as previously mentioned, copyright laws vary across markets. In the USA, the term of copyright in sound recordings is ninety-five years. So, if a brand attempts to use an American controlled recording of a younger date and claim it's public domain in the UK, you can expect a legal claim. Similarly, if you attempt to use an EU State controlled recording aged between seventy and ninety-five years in an online campaign that's visible in the USA, again you can expect a claim.

If all this seems difficult and complex, it is. So what's the take out for brands?

- **Never assume that a song or recording is out of copyright and available to use freely, even if your agency claims it is.**
- **For any use related to brand marketing, music rights owners will, wherever possible, try to claim a title is still in copyright in order to extract a licence fee.**
- **Always get assistance from a suitably qualified expert or music lawyer before relying on any form of out of copyright / public domain protection as a means to avoid paying licence fees.**

- **It will always be cheaper to check copyright status first than to take a risk and pay penalty fees afterwards.**

Chapter summary

In this chapter we've examined the legal distinction between songs and recordings which is essential for marketers to grasp if they're to take greater control of music licensing. We've learned about:

- **The rights of composers, lyricists and songwriters**
- **The rights of featured and non-featured artists**
- **The issues involved when using re-records or cover versions**
- **The complexities surrounding public domain status**

As you read through this book, it might be useful to jot down some notes to record your thoughts.

Reader's notes

(i) Big Mental Note

(ii) One Big Step

CHAPTER 2
The difference between music publishers and record labels

Having explained the distinction between songs and recordings, in this chapter we'll examine the rights owners who typically control them; music publishers and record labels.

You've now learned about the fundamental difference between songs and recordings. It's essential that all marketers who use commercial catalogue music in their campaigns appreciate this distinction. So, as a buyer, if you're going to license these separate rights, you need to know who the sellers are. In general terms:

- **Music publishers control music and lyrics** (on behalf of songwriters)
- **Music publishers control compositions** (on behalf of composers)
- **Record labels control sound recordings** (on behalf of featured recording artists)

Note that I said <u>featured</u> recording artists above. That's because the rights of the non-featured artists (or session musicians) are often licensed by their performers union.

There are exceptions to the above, the obvious ones being:

- **Unpublished songwriters and composers control their own works**
  This is a key tenet of copyright law. The creator controls their work until they assign it elsewhere.
- **Unsigned recording artists may control their own recordings**
  Generally speaking, in copyright law, the party who paid for the recording session owns that recording – though they don't necessarily have the right to commercially exploit it without a contract with the artist. In the 1980s and 1990s, for an unsigned artist, that party might have been their manager or a record producer working speculatively. However, given it's been possible for at least a decade to make a perfectly decent record with nothing more than a laptop and a microphone, most unsigned artists will control their own recordings.

(i) Historical background

This won't be a detailed history lesson, but for a marketer there are a few useful points to know:

Music Publishers

- **Music publishing is much older than the record industry**
- **Origins date back to the fifteenth century, but developed formally from eighteenth century**

- **Initially based on the sale of sheet music for several centuries**
- **Publishers licensed piano rolls in nineteenth century**
- **Publishers felt threatened by advent of sound recording in late nineteenth century**
- **Development of the "mechanical right" – the right to mechanically reproduce the music and words of compositions onto sound recordings**
- **Mechanical licences for wax cylinders, 78rpm discs, vinyl, CDs, downloads**

I spent nearly ten years working in music publishing during the 1990s and early 2000s and have a particular fondness for the industry. My general observations are:

- **Historically, many music publishers started as family businesses**
- **Stalwarts remain independent, but many have been acquired by larger groups**
- **Publishers have a deep emotional attachment to their song catalogue**
- **This is separate from and outlives the relationship with the songwriters**
- **Music publishing is often seen as the less sexy end of the music industry**
- **Music publishing is rarely understood properly by record labels**
- **Music publishers have a history of adapting to new technology**
- **Ultimately their business is to license their copyrights in return for money**
- **Music publishers will probably outlive record labels**

The key point you need to know as a marketer:

Whatever version of a song you want to use, you must get a licence from the music publisher that controls it.

In the market of licensing music to brands, music publishers have more power than record labels, as you can always re-record a song or possibly find a cover version if you can't license the original artist recording.

Record Labels
The division between the careers of songwriters and artists is understood to have changed with The Beatles. Before then, artists were perhaps just entertainers or even "turns" – their careers might be short, but it was the songwriters and their publishers that had the real power.

That changed in the 1960s and continued certainly through to 2000. During this period, record labels were seen as the dominant force in the music industry. Financially, their profits were far larger than music publishers given that the record label's share of each physical unit sold vastly exceeded that paid out to the artist ("artist royalty") and the music publisher ("mechanical royalty"). This reached its climax from the early 1980s to 2000 when record labels sold CDs at a higher price than vinyl though with lower associated manufacturing costs. Vast profits were made which fuelled the well documented hedonistic excesses of the recording industry. In this period, touring was still a potentially loss making exercise to promote album sales. With such large profits, record labels could afford to take huge risks on new acts – hence the anecdotal label practice of; "Sign ten artists, lose money on nine and make it all back and more on the tenth".

Of course the internet changed everything. Nearly twenty years on, the current trends are:

- **Income from the sale of recorded music is often a minor part of artists' total revenue**
- **Income from the sale of downloads from services such as iTunes and Amazon appears to have peaked and didn't replace the fall in revenue from CDs.**
- **Excluding superstar artists, recordings are often little more than a calling card**
- **Emerging artists will often give away recordings for free as a promotional item**
- **Recordings promote tours and merchandise**
- **Digital music streaming services such as Spotify and Deezer were hailed by many as the next development beyond downloads and have gained traction in some markets, particularly Sweden. The subsequent launch of Apple Music demonstrates that the mighty Cupertino company also sees streaming in the same way.**
- **Frequent complaints from recording artists, songwriters and their trade bodies about the tiny income they receive from streaming.**

So, what does this mean for record labels?

- **Declining market for sale of recorded music on a per unit basis**
- **Smaller margins**
- **Risk averse attitude to signing new artists**
- **Far fewer artists signed, on much lower advances**
- **Less artist development, as this role now falls to managers**
- **Attempts to claw income from other sources (live, publishing, brand partnerships) via so-called "360 Deals" with new recording artists**

What are the other key takeouts:

- **Record labels have a real need to monetise their recordings**
- **They look to brands as a vital source of revenue**
- **All labels now have dedicated sync licensing teams**
- **Larger labels have brand partnership teams**
- **Labels are re-calibrating their place in the music industry given that the live sector is now much more powerful**

The key point you need to know as a marketer:

For record labels, what was once just "secondary income" is now a key element of their business i.e. the licensing of recordings into commercials and branded online video (known as synchronisation or "sync") is of fundamental importance to record labels. Carefully managed, brands and agencies can use this as leverage in negotiation.

Inherent Conflict

The fragmented music industry has always been riddled with internal conflict. That's why until the launch of trade body UK Music, the music business hasn't had a unified lobbying voice within government. UK Music positions itself as a campaigning and lobbying group which represents every part of the recorded and live music industry. It's supported by all the individual trade bodies which represent independent and major record labels, music publishers, artist managers, session musicians, songwriters, record producers, featured recording artists, booking agents, promoters, music venues and festivals.

To explain the inherent conflict:

Record labels believe they deserve the lion's share of profits from any exploitation of a sound recording that embodies the song. Music publishers obviously disagree.

There's a fundamental imbalance between the division of monies between record labels and music publishers from

(i) The sale of recorded music – where the record label receives the vast majority

Versus

(ii) Synchronisation licensing – where typically it's split 50/50

There's an on-going debate about downloads and streaming whereby publishers are trying to claim a much larger slice of revenue.

Why does this matter for marketers?

It reinforces the need to form strong relationships with music publishers, because they have more power than record labels in the sync licensing market.

(ii) Roles and responsibilities

I've mentioned sync and synchronisation a number of times – We'll examine this in more detail in the next chapter, but as a marketer you need to understand that this means the act of synchronising music (song and recording) against moving images. That's what you do when you (or your agency) dub music onto your commercial or online video i.e. putting audio to visual content.

When considering the roles of music publishers and record labels, what does synchronisation mean for marketers?

Music Publishers

- **Music publishers grant sync licences for songs on behalf of their songwriters.**
- **Music publishers have a responsibility to secure the songwriter's prior approval to associate the songwriter's creation with a brand (which wasn't the original purpose of the song)**
- **Music publishers must warrant that they have the right to grant the licence and own or administer the song they are licensing.**
- **Music publishers must warrant that the song is wholly original and doesn't**

infringe the rights of third parties.

- **Music publishers must indemnify the licensee (that's your brand or your agency) against their breach of that warranty.**

Record Labels

- **Record labels grant sync licences for recordings on behalf of their featured artists.**
- **Record labels have a responsibility to secure the featured artist's prior approval to associate the recording with a brand (which wasn't the original purpose of the recording)**
- **Record labels must warrant that they have the right to grant the licence and own or administer the recording they are licensing.**
- **Record labels must warrant that the recording is wholly original and doesn't infringe the rights of third parties.**
- **Record labels must indemnify the licensee (that's your brand or your agency) against their breach of that warranty.**

Watch Out:

A key note on warranties and indemnities: Whilst music publishers and record labels should always include a licensor's warranty in their licences, it is common practice to limit the indemnity to the level of sync licence fee paid by the brand or its agency, the licensee. This is deeply unpopular with many brands' corporate in-house legal teams who are often astounded that music rights owners adopt such a stance.

Chapter summary

In this chapter we've examined the different roles of music publishers and record labels. We've learned that:

- **Music publishers control songs and compositions**
- **Music publishers license "publishing rights" to brands and ad agencies**
- **Record labels control sound recordings**
- **Record labels license "master rights" to brands and ad agencies**
- **Music publishers and record labels aren't always aligned**

Reader's notes

(i) Big Mental Note

(ii) One Big Step

CHAPTER 3
The role of performers' unions

*In the previous chapter we examined how record labels license
the rights of featured artists on sound recordings. In this
chapter, we'll examine how the rights of non-featured artists
are licensed by performers unions.*

We previously discussed the distinction between featured and non-featured artists as they may appear on an existing sound recording. Note that "non-featured artist" includes "session musicians" and "backing singers".

Quick Recap

Featured artists

- **Typically exclusively signed to record label**
- **Record label grants sync rights in master sound recording**
- **These sync rights include recorded performance of featured artist**

Non-featured artists

- **Not exclusively signed to record label**
- **Record label grants sync rights in master sound recording**
- **These sync rights do not include recorded performance of non-featured artists unless their rights have been bought out**
- **The situation varies by market**

In some markets, for example the UK and USA, when non-featured artists are engaged to perform on a studio session recording, they grant rights to the record label under a template agreement between their union and the trade body to which the featured artist's record label belongs.

Usually the template agreement grants rights to exploit the recording for commercial sale to the public but it does *not* include sync rights which have to be licensed separately from the performers union. Any secondary or sync usage, such as for commercials or branded online video, requires additional fees for each non-featured artist.

What does this mean for marketers?

The challenge is to:

- **Establish who controls the sync rights in the recorded performance of non-featured artists in the specific sound recording you wish to use**
- **Non-featured artists can be both session musicians and backing singers, each of which may be represented by different performers unions**

- **Approach those parties with a clear summary of the required usage**
- **Secure their quote, which is usually a fixed rate per non-featured artist**

This can be a complex task for which smart marketers seek external expert support.

Chapter summary

In this chapter we've examined the how the rights of non-featured artists in sound recordings are licensed for brand campaigns. We've learned that:

- **Record labels don't always control the rights of non-featured artists**
- **Record labels don't always have information on those non-featured artists**
- **It is the responsibility of the brand (or their agency) to license the rights of non-featured artists from the performers union who represent them**

Reader's notes

(i) Big Mental Note

(ii) One Big Step

CHAPTER 4
The role of artist managers and booking agents

*Having looked at the function of music rights owners,
principally music publishers and record labels, in this chapter
we'll examine the role of the artist manager who's closest to
the artist in all aspects of their career. We'll also look at the
booking agent who's solely focused on live performance.*

As a marketer, you probably understand the landscape when dealing with on-screen talent, whether that be an actor or a model. They have an agent, one person or company, who represents them. There might possibly be a lawyer involved, but essentially there's one contracting party – the on-screen talent.

In music, it's completely different as even a solo artist wears many hats and has different representatives for the different aspects of their career:

Career Aspect	Interests represented by
Recording Artist	Record label
Songwriter	Music Publisher
Live Performer	Booking Agent
Brand ambassador	Manager or record label
Name, image, likeness	Record label or manager

The above is a guide and there will always be exceptions. However, let's say you want to:

- **Book an artist to play at your brand's event**
- **Film the show and post it on your brand's YouTube Channel**
- **Have the artist do some "meet and greets" with competition winners**
- **Have the artist promote the event on their own social media channels**
- **Have the artist do a photo op with your CEO which you can post online**

The above wish list is not uncommon yet it involves negotiations with all four of the above representatives (label, publisher, manager, agent) and often they have divergent agendas.

We've learned in detail about the roles of music publishers and record labels, so now let's look at the roles of the artist manager and booking agent:

(i) Artist managers

Artist managers have (or are supposed to have) the artist's best interests in mind across every element of their career. The artist manager often performs the role of professional advisor, confidante, relationship counsellor, advocate, substitute parent, nanny, mentor and sometimes minder. It's a very tough job and ultimately relies on mutual trust and respect. If that breaks down, the relationship ceases to work irrespective of any contract.

The manager may have represented the artist since the start of their career – initially working for love rather than financial reward, sometimes for many years. In this role, the manager may have negotiated the artist's exclusive record and publishing contracts, signing away rights in return for financial advances and marketing support.

Increasingly, emerging artists who sign exclusive recording agreements with major record labels relinquish some rights or sometimes a share of income beyond that from the copyright in sound recordings. However, in the first instance it's always worth approaching the artist's manager if you want the artist to:

- **Endorse your brand by appearing in an advertising campaign**
- **Become a brand ambassador**
- **Create and record a new song for a campaign**
- **Create a new cover recording for a campaign**
- **Perform at an event**
- **Attend an event**

- **Promote your brand via the artist's social media channels**
- **Allow their name, image or likeness to be used to promote your brand**

The manager is best placed to discuss with the artist whether or not they wish to be involved and also advise whether they can even grant the necessary rights.

Watch-outs

It's not unheard of for managers to claim they can grant all the rights you might need as they want to take all the money on the table. However, from the above wish list it's likely that:

- **The creation of a new recording requires an artist waiver and master sync licence from the artist's record label *in addition to* an engagement agreement with the artist.**
- **The creation of a new song requires a publishing sync licence from the artist's music publisher *in addition to* an engagement agreement with the artist.**
- **If the artist co-writes a song with other another independent songwriter, known as a "co-writer", the co-writer may have a separate music publisher. If so, a separate publishing sync licence is required for the co-writer's share of the song.**
- **Any live performance may need to be negotiated with a live booking agent (see next section on Booking Agents)**
- **Any use of name, image or likeness may require a licence from the artist's record label; if the label has this right it will be part of the artist waiver, rather than the master sync licence.**

It's also not uncommon for record labels to claim that they can grant a very broad set of artist's rights, particularly image, brand endorsement, brand ambassadorship and even live performance, when in reality these are not controlled on an exclusive basis.

So, as a brand marketer, you need to be wary and cross check the claims of each party to ensure you are dealing with the actual owner of the specific rights you need. To be one step removed will result in over-payment.

(ii) Booking agents

Once an artist reaches the level of performing in decent sized venues, it's likely they'll have a booking agent. By decent sized, let's assume anything with a 500+ capacity.

A traditional music-industry booking agent will have the exclusive right to book live performances for the artist in specific territories, which usually includes branded events. To clarify, the booking agent can only negotiate the live performance – not any other rights which may be controlled by the artist, their record label, music publisher or any other third parties.

What does this mean for marketers?

- Booking agents usually work on commission, in the 10% – 15% range
- So, they're solely incentivised by the performance fee
- They don't care about other promotional benefits the brand brings to the artist

- **They won't help you secure artist waivers or sync licences if you film the show**
- **They'll try to insist you use their standard booking contract**
- **You should insist that the artist countersigns the contract**

Beyond traditional music industry booking agents are the much larger US talent agents who've set up shop in the UK. Creative Artists Agency ("CAA") and William Morris Endeavour ("WME") are two obvious examples. These agents not only broker deals for artists' live performances but are also very active in the brand endorsement and partnership market. Their mind set is informed by the representation of Hollywood stars who command top dollar for brand endorsement deals. That said, their rights to broker brand partnership deals for musical artists might not always be exclusive so it's always worth speaking to the artist's manager first.

Chapter summary

In this chapter we've examined the key role of the artist manager in securing the approvals that brands need to use existing music tracks or to work with an artist. We've learned that artist managers:

- **are closest to the artist**
- **have 360 degree vision of the artist's career**
- **secure the approvals that publishers and labels need to grant sync licences**
- **may be able to directly negotiate name, image and likeness rights**
- **usually negotiate brand ambassador and endorsement rights**

- **may try to claim ownership of rights already granted elsewhere**
- **may not be fully aligned with the artist's music publisher and record label**

We've also learned that most established artists have booking agents who:

- **have the exclusive right to negotiate live performance agreements**
- **are solely incentivised by commission on performance fees**
- **have no financial reward from other aspects of the artist's career**

Reader's notes

(i) Big Mental Note

(ii) One Big Step

SECTION TWO
Which rights do brands need to license?

CHAPTER 5
Know your rights

In Section One we examined the key distinction between songs / "publishing rights" and recordings / "master rights" as respectively controlled by music publishers and recording labels. However, these fundamentally different copyrights are further sub-divided into synchronisation, performing, mechanical and dubbing rights which aren't all licensed by the same bodies. In this chapter we'll look at how this works.

(i) Synchronisation rights

By now you should have grasped that, as a marketer, synchronisation or "sync" is the main right you need to understand. So, what is it?

It's the act of dubbing music (song and/or recording) against moving images; putting audio to visual.

As soon as you contemplate using music against a commercial or video, there's a need to secure sync licences *before* you exploit that content.

Anomaly: Radio

Commercial catalogue music used in radio campaigns still has to be licensed even though there are no moving images. These licences are typically brokered with the sync teams of record labels and music publishers although no actual "sync" takes place.

(ii) Performing rights

Confusingly, this *isn't* about the engagement of artists for live performances. It is instead about the public performance of songs and sound recordings. So how does that work?

Songs

- Broadcast transmission (TV, Radio)
- Online transmission (audio-visual or audio only)
- Commercial premises (retail space, offices, pubs, clubs)
- Audio playback (concert halls, music venues, sports arenas, pop-up venues)
- Live performance (concert halls, music venues, sports arenas, pop-up venues)

Recordings

- Broadcast transmission (TV, Radio)
- Online transmission (audio-visual or audio only)

- Commercial premises (retail space, offices, pubs, clubs)
- Audio playback (concert halls, music venues, sports arenas, pop-up venues)

Spot the key difference?

There is a public performance right in songs as *performed live* in concert halls, music venues, sports arena and pop-up venues. However, in a live performance, the audience isn't hearing a recording (unless the performers use backing tracks) so the public performance right in recordings isn't relevant.

Who grants the licences?

In the UK, performing rights are licensed by two key "collection societies" or "performing right organisations" (PROs) as they're more commonly known:

(1) Performing Rights Society ("PRS" or "PRS for Music"):
who license songs (on behalf of composers, songwriters & music publishers)

(2) Phonographic Performance Ltd ("PPL"):
who license sound recordings (on behalf of performers and record labels)

Outside the UK, each market has its own equivalents of PRS for Music and PPL.

What does this mean for marketers?

Broadcast

Advertisers buy media air time from broadcasters in order to transmit TV and Radio commercials to the target audience – This is clearly "bought" media. In some cases, brands might also secure placement of their content within editorial TV and Radio programming, for example a programme about advertising and/or the music used within it – This would be considered "earned" media. In both cases in the UK, it's the broadcaster rather than the advertiser who pays blanket performing right licence fees to PRS for Music and PPL. This is entirely separate from the sync licence fees the brand pays to music publishers and record labels. So, you don't need to worry about performing right / public performance licence fees from a marketing budget perspective – it's the broadcaster's responsibility as they, not the brand, are broadcasting your content.

Online transmission

In the UK, if you host any music on your company's corporate website, whether that's audio only or audio-visual, you <u>do</u> need a blanket PRS for Music licence to cover all the applicable songs. The type of licence varies, but it's often called a General Entertainment Streaming Licence. The fee paid is determined by the number of songs and the volume of streams. It is your responsibility to secure this, as it's your company's website. Depending on the songs used, PRS for Music may be able to grant you a licence covering the European Union ("EU"), which is generally the case for "Anglo-American" repertoire. Outside the EU, there's an obligation to secure further licences on a market-by-market basis unless your content is geo-locked (see Section 3, Chapter 11).

For any third party websites, it is the responsibility of the site owner to have the relevant licence in place with PRS for Music. At the time of writing, YouTube has such a licence although its commercial terms are confidential. However, Facebook does not have a licence with PRS for Music and tries to place the onus on brands to secure one. The question for brands is, how do you make your videos safely available on Facebook or any other third-party side? The answer is to embed links to YouTube, which means that your content is visible on, for example, unlicensed Facebook although it's being streamed from licensed YouTube where the video is actually hosted.

Key anomaly

In the UK, PPL can't grant blanket performing right licences for sound recordings for online usage by brands. Instead, this right should be granted by record labels within the terms of master sync licences.

Commercial Premises

In the UK, if your brand is a "bricks and mortar" retailer, your company needs blanket PRS & PPL licences for all its stores in which music can be heard. This usually falls under the remit of corporate Procurement teams who may broker licences directly with PRS and PPL or outsource it to a third-party supplier. So, although it's a cost to your company, it's not usually a concern for the marketing department. The same is true of music played in your offices, which also requires PRS and PPL blanket licences, though many companies fail to recognise this. Outside the UK, the international affiliates of PRS and PPL have a similar role.

Audio Playback

This is always the responsibility of the venue owner. So, if you're hosting an event in an existing venue, check the venue owner has valid PRS & PPL licences in place. However, if you're creating a temporary pop-up venue for a branded event, it is your responsibility to secure blanket PRS & PPL licences for that venue – even if it's just for one day. Outside the UK, the international affiliates of PRS and PPL have a similar role.

Live Performance

This only relates to PRS but the same rules apply as for Audio Playback. If you're hiring a venue, it's the owner's responsibility to have a PRS licence. If you're creating a pop-up venue, it's your responsibility. Outside the UK, the international affiliates of PRS have a similar role.

In all the above cases, the general rule of thumb is this: Whoever is responsible for the actual "public performance" of the song or recording, they must secure the public performance licence(s) and pay the appropriate licence fee(s).

(iii) Mechanical / Reproduction rights

If you create copies of songs or recordings to give away to consumers, you need licences in place from the rights owners, typically music publishers and record labels. These licences usually attract a per unit royalty in return for the grant of:

Mechanical licence: for songs
Reproduction / dubbing licence: for sound recordings

In both cases, prior permission is required from the rights owners.

In the 1990s, many brands created promotional "Premium CDs" which were licensed this way. In the early 2000s, many brands created promotional ringtones or downloads which were also licensed this way. Now, it's far less common as consumers can access all the music they want via streaming services on an ad-funded or subscription basis. So, why would consumers want a free download unless it was completely exclusive content?

Marketers need to remember that:
Brands cannot freely distribute music on any format, whether Vinyl, CD or digital download unless they have the appropriate licences from the rights owners and have paid the necessary fees which are usually a royalty per unit.

Chapter summary

In this chapter we've examined how the copyright in songs / "publishing rights and sound recordings / "master rights" are further sub-divided into different rights.

For songs, we've learned about:

- **Synchronisation ("sync") right – use with moving images**
- **Sync licences are usually granted by music publishers**
- **Performing right – broadcast, on-line, commercial premises, concerts**
- **Performing right licences are granted in the UK by PRS for Music**
- **Mechanical right – copying to vinyl, CD or download**

- **Mechanical right licences are granted in UK by the publisher or PRS for Music**

For sound recordings, we've learned about:

- **Synchronisation ("sync") right – use with moving images**
- **Sync licences are usually granted by record labels**
- **Performing right – broadcast, commercial premises**
- **Performing right licences are granted in the UK by PPL**
- **Dubbing – copying to vinyl, CD or download**
- **Dubbing right licences are granted in the UK by PPL (usually limited to in-store usage) or directly by record labels**

Reader's notes

(i) Big Mental Note

(ii) One Big Step

SECTION THREE

How much? Cost drivers and cost management

Now we've gained an understanding of how music rights work, I'm going to show you how to efficiently buy those rights. To achieve this, you'll need to learn the key cost drivers involved and how to balance the scales between buyer and seller.

CHAPTER 6
Approval chains

In this chapter we'll examine why most music publishers and record labels can't immediately provide a definitive answer to sync licence requests from brands or ad agencies. The reason? There are usually approval parties and, in some cases, longer approval chains involving multiple parties.

Brands looking to license commercial catalogue music often come unstuck as they fail to appreciate the timescales needed for clearance. Why? They don't understand the number of parties involved in the approval chain. We'll now look at how this works which will inform your production timing plans.

Licence Request – Outbound Process

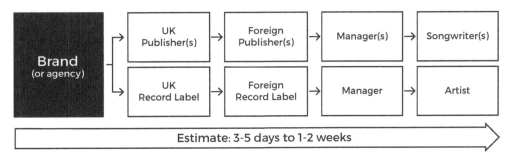

Approval or Denial – Inbound Process

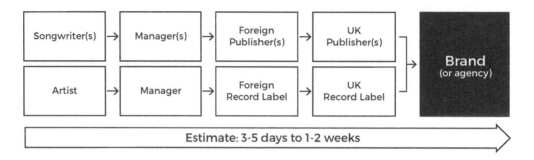

(i) Licensee location

Firstly, let's refresh ourselves on some terminology:

Licensee: The buyer – The brand or its agency

Licensor: The seller – The music rights owner (music publisher and/or record label)

The location of the licensee entity dictates the market (or "territory" in music licensing jargon) in which the deal must be brokered.

Let's say you work for the UK subsidiary of an American Corporation. The UK subsidiary is likely to be a UK registered company. Therefore, your UK company will need to broker music licences with the UK subsidiaries of the music rights owners who control the music track you want *irrespective of the location of the original rights owners or nationality of the artist or songwriters.*

Yes, I know that's a bit complex, so let me explain using a real life example:

In 2013, Taylor Swift appeared in a Diet Coke commercial which featured the title "22" from her "Red" album". Taylor Swift is of course an American artist and The Coca Cola Company (TCCC") which owns Diet Coke is headquartered in Atlanta, Georgia, USA. It's therefore a reasonable assumption that this deal was brokered in America.

Ignoring the artist's actual appearance in the commercial, let's consider the music title "22" – specifically the sound recording. As an artist, Taylor Swift is signed to Big Machine Records in America who control the recording of "22". This is licensed through Universal Music in the UK who have the right, subject to the artist's approval, to grant sync licences for this recording for use by brands.

Let's consider now what would happen if the Diet Coke campaign had been created by TCCC in the UK and not, as I've assumed, the head office in Atlanta, Georgia. Looking specifically at the sound recording, the process would be:

- **TCCC UK must approach Universal Music UK with a master sync licence request**
- **Universal Music UK refers the request to Universal Music USA**
- **Universal Music USA refers the request to Big Machine Records**
- **Big Machine Records refers the request to Taylor Swift's management**

The key point here is this:

Even though both the artist and the brand is American, if the campaign originates in another market (e.g. the UK), the local office of the brand (or its agency) has to approach the local record label that controls the recording in that market. TCCC UK could not directly approach Big Machine Records in the USA but instead must approach Universal Music UK as the local record label. The market in which the campaign originates determines the market in which the music must be licensed, even if it's on a global basis.

(ii) Local licensors

Looking at the previous diagram, you'll start to understand how the approval chain works.

We established that, if you're working for a UK registered company, it's your office or agency that must be the licensee if you're commissioning the campaign.

The local licensors will be the UK offices of the record label and music publisher(s) who control the title you want to use. They could have one of two roles:

- **They're probably the original rights owner if the nationality of the songwriter / artist is British.**

or

- **They're probably just licensing rights on behalf of an overseas rights owner if the nationality of the songwriter / artist isn't British.**

The key word is "probably" because there are exceptions to the above:

- **Some British artists sign record deals directly with record labels in the USA or Europe. The same can be true for British songwriters with American and European music publishers.**
- **Some European or American artists sign record deals with UK record labels. The same can be true for European or American songwriters with UK music publishers.**

What does this mean for marketers?

You need to establish early on if the UK record label and music publisher you've approached are the original rights owners who deal directly with the music talent, or if they're acting on behalf of overseas rights owners. In the latter case, UK record labels and music publishers will likely have the ability to act on behalf of overseas rights owners once their approval has been granted.

(iii) Copyright owner / Approval party

We've established that you need to approach the local UK offices of the relevant record label and music publisher – but in most cases they can't just immediately agree a deal with you. Any quote they provide will be marked "subject to approval". There are number of potential scenarios here:

- **The local UK record label or music publisher actually owns the copyright but the British artist or songwriter has the prior right of approval for sync licences.**

- **The local UK record label or music publisher just administers the rights of the British artist or songwriter whose own UK company is the original rights owner and has prior right of approval for sync licences.**
- **The local UK record label or music publisher just administers the rights of an overseas affiliate who in turn controls rights on behalf of an overseas artist or songwriter. The overseas affiliate has prior right of approval for sync licences.**

It's safe to assume that whoever you approach with a licence request will always need to seek someone else's permission. There are examples with older catalogue, e.g. pre-1970 where this isn't the case, but this is less common. So, there will almost always be an approval party who may one of the following:

- **An artist or songwriter**
- **The estate of a deceased artist or songwriter**
- **A manager or lawyer acting for an artist or songwriter, or their estate**
- **An "original rights owner" who controls rights on behalf of an artist or songwriter, or their estate**

(iv) Artist and management

It's uncommon for sync licensing teams within record labels and music publishers to deal directly with established artists and songwriters. Licensing teams usually liaise with the managers of those artists and songwriters.

The manager typically handles all aspects of their client's career, acting as a filter for incoming licence requests, especially ones for brand campaigns. The manager will immediately know if the "fit" feels right. For example, if their artist is an ardent vegetarian, they will immediately deny a request for any meat-based product or brand. They wouldn't risk offending their artist by presenting the request. Similarly, if an artist is below the legal drinking age or has had problems with alcohol addiction, the manager will know not to present any licence requests for alcoholic beverage brands – the requests would just be denied.

So, let's assume that the manager considers your request sufficiently worthy to present to the artist. Will you get an immediate answer? No, almost certainly not.

Established artists and songwriters are busy people. You need to consider that they might be:

- **On tour**
- **In the recording studio**
- **Shooting a video**
- **In writing sessions**

Given that established artists probably make more money now through touring rather than sales of recorded music, being away on tour is the more likely option.

It's quite probable that it might be several days before the artist gets to see your request. They may be eight hours behind or ten hours ahead. Their tour manager has to pick the right moment to present a bundle of licence requests to a jet lagged artist on the tour bus or plane between shows. Will your request stand out? Will the artist look on it favourably? Of course that depends on:

- **The brand**
- **The usage**
- **The offered fee**

What's the take-out for marketers?

Remember to leave plenty of time as artists and songwriters will, at the very least, take a few days to respond and sometimes several weeks.

Chapter summary

In this chapter we've examined how the process of securing songwriter and artist approvals for sync licences can be lengthy and complex. We've learned that:

- **Brands are licensees, music rights owners are licensors**
- **The market in which licensee is located dictates the licensor they approach**
- **The licensor will almost always have an approval party**
- **The approval party may be the songwriter or artist**
- **The approval party may be a separate overseas copyright owner**
- **The approval party has the absolute right of approval**
- **Brands should allow a minimum of one week for approvals**
- **Brands should expect that approval may take much longer**
- **Brands should have a back-up plan in the event of a licence denial**

Reader's notes

(i) Big Mental Note

(ii) One Big Step

CHAPTER 7
Fame and stature

In this chapter we'll discover how songs sometimes have a life of their own and tend to be immune to changes in the reputation of their songwriters. In contrast, the value of sound recordings is more closely linked with the reputation of recording artists.

Fame can be fickle, though it tends to affect artists more than songwriters. Think of it as an index, like the FTSE100.

(i) Songs and songwriters

The beauty of music publishing is that great songs live forever – or at least it can seem that way. These songs are often called "classics", "standards" or "evergreen copyrights". Songs like these tend to have been recorded and performed by many different artists and so command a huge premium in the sync licensing market. Given that in most EU States the life of copyright in songs is seventy years after the death of the songwriter, this high value lasts a long time. As a few examples, think of the amazing song catalogues of Cole Porter ("Night & Day", "I Get A Kick Out Of You"), Rodgers and Hammerstein ("Oh What A Beautiful Morning", "The Surrey With A Fringe On Top") and Bacharach and David ("Raindrops Keep Falling On My Head, "I Say A Little Prayer"). I'd argue that their songs will still be famous in another fifty years and possibly longer. Of course they will eventually fall out of copyright, but while they're in copyright the market value of those songs and their songwriters will remain very high in the sync licensing market.

What does this mean for marketers?

Even for current songwriters, the perceived value of their songs is often not affected by the ups and downs of their careers as artists (if the songwriter is also an artist). The songs have a life of their own, especially when covered by another artist.

(ii) Recordings and artists

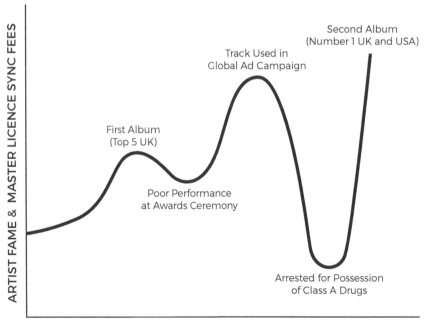

The value of recordings is more likely to vary with the peaks and troughs in the artist's career, compared with the songs written by the same person.

With social media able to report and instantly share the slightest misdemeanour of a famous artist, brands have to consider possible reputational damage by association. The popular media loves to build artists up then knock them down, so bad behaviour is newsworthy. If a brand is negotiating the use of a recording by an artist who's exposed in this way, arguably the value of that recording may fall if far fewer brands are brave enough to still use it. However, sometimes it can go the other way, where notoriety increases the value. It depends on the brand and whether it seeks or recoils from the edginess associated with some artists.

In addition to artist behaviour, sales of the artist's recorded music will affect sync value. Let's consider the "difficult second album" syndrome. It's not uncommon for tracks from a successful first album to attract a high value in the sync market, especially where that album achieved gold* or platinum* status and/or a top five position in the album charts. However, where the second album fails to live up to sales expectations, those newer recordings are likely to attract lower sync fees, especially as both artist and record label will be very keen to secure the exposure from brand campaigns.

In the UK, currently sales of 100,000 albums denotes gold status and 300,000 albums denotes platinum status as certified by the British Phonographic Industry ("BPI").

What does this mean for marketers?

If you're looking to use a recording by a current artist, ask yourself, "Are they darlings of the media or in the dog house for recent bad behaviour?"

If you're looking to use a recording by an established artist, where are they in the arc of their career? Would a brand campaign help to rejuvenate interest in their catalogue?

Consider these points carefully to understand the leverage that you have with the record label who controls the sound recording you wish to license.

Given that some music artists occasionally indulge in anti-social or even illegal behaviour, it's wise to have "death and disgrace" insurance in place to mitigate risk should you need to rapidly terminate an artist relationship or use of their music track.

Chapter summary

In this chapter we've looked at how the changing reputation of songwriters and artists respectively affects the value of their songs and recordings in different ways. We've learned that:

- **Songs, especially famous ones, have a life of their own**
- **The value of songs can be immune to the songwriter's reputation**
- **Recordings are more closely linked to artist who made them**
- **The value of recordings may fluctuate with the artist's reputation**
- **Brands should be aware of an artist's career cycle to understand value**

Reader's notes

(i) Big Mental Note

(ii) One Big Step

CHAPTER 8
Exclusivity

*In this chapter we'll explain how brands are able to secure
limited levels of exclusivity in the sync licences they secure
from music rights owners.*

You might assume that when you broker a sync licence for a song or recording, particularly for a high fee, you're automatically protected from competitors using the same music. That assumption would be wrong.

Virtually all standard sync licences for commercial catalogue titles are non-exclusive meaning that your direct competitors can run simultaneous campaigns in the same markets with the same music.

So, how do you protect yourself? The answer is to add a level of exclusivity to the deal, but of course this comes at a cost. The following graph explains this point.

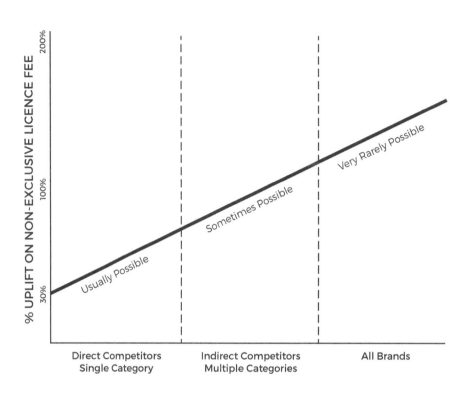

(i) Single product category

Let's say you're in the marketing team for Johnnie Walker whisky. You're negotiating a sync licence for a music track and want to prevent competitor whisky brands using the same music. Assuming you're able to secure clearance for the track you want for use by an alcoholic beverage brand, then exclusivity within the whisky category would be classed "single product category".

It's wise to negotiate an option for single product category exclusivity based on a percentage uplift on the non-exclusive licence fee. You might want to offer a 25% – 30% uplift but the rights owners could counter-offer at 50% or even higher.

Should you agree terms and exercise the exclusivity option when the deal commences, it's important to remember that exclusivity is limited to:

- **Licensed Term (or extensions thereof) i.e. duration of licence**
- **Licensed Territory (or "markets" in your language)**
- **Licensed Media (or "channels" in your language)**

If you're only running a UK TV campaign for 6 months, you're only protected in the UK, for that 6 month period, and just for TV. You'll have no exclusivity before the campaign starts or after it ends.

Key Point: Online

There's a general exception to exclusivity which catches out many marketers. Almost all music rights owners will refuse to grant any exclusivity for online usage. So, even if you manage to secure exclusivity for an above-the-line usage such as TV, the online element of your campaign won't have the same protection.

(ii) Multiple product category

Keeping with the Johnnie Walker example, you might want broader protection covering all alcoholic beverage brands, not just whisky. Many music rights owners will refuse to grant this as the alcoholic beverage sector is a heavy music user and hence a strong revenue source. The perspective of music publishers and record labels will always be, "Why should I grant this protection and jeopardise income from other campaigns?".

The only answer is of course a very significant uplift on the non-exclusive sync licence fee to justify what music rights owners will see as a gamble. As a marketer, you can expect to pay an uplift of 70% – 150% for multiple product category exclusivity <u>over and above</u> the non-exclusive licence fee.

(iii) Songs versus recordings

Marketers often ask, "Do I need exclusivity for both song and recording?". It's a good question; you need to consider this:

Song
Exclusivity for the song will, by default, also cover any sound recordings of that song.

Recording
Exclusivity for the recording, will only cover that specific recording of the song.

What should you do?

If you're licensing a track where the songwriter and artist is the same person, both publishing and master sync licence requests will probably be sent along the separate approval chains to one manager. That manager will therefore have visibility of both deals. If there's exclusivity in the publishing licence (with an applicable uplift in fee), the manager will demand the same for the master licence. In other words, absolute parity between the two licences, which is known as Most Favoured Nations or "MFN" – I'll explain this in more detail in Section 3, Chapter 10.

If you're licensing a well-known song covered by a less established artist, the position is rather different and more complex. In these situations it would be wise to seek advice from a suitably qualified expert.

Chapter summary

In this chapter we've discovered that sync licences granted by music rights owners are non-exclusive by default. This means that direct competitors can simultaneously use the same song and/or recording in the same market as your campaign.

We've learned that exclusivity:

- **must be negotiated in advance as an add-on to the main licence**
- **will almost always command an up-lift on the non-exclusive licence fee**
- **will be limited to the licensed term, territory and off-line media**
- **will almost always exclude online media**
- **may be granted for direct competitors in a single product category**
- **may be granted for indirect competitors in multiple product categories**
- **is very rarely granted to cover all advertised brands**

Reader's notes

(i) Big Mental Note

(ii) One Big Step

CHAPTER 9
Usage

In this chapter we'll examine the three key pillars of usage:
Term, Territory and Media and their effect on licence fees,
together with context of use.

When brands use third party controlled intellectual property rights in their campaigns, usage is one of the key cost drivers. This applies to music, on-screen talent, photography, stock images and clips, indeed any IP controlled by 3rd parties. Remember that you are essentially renting someone else's equity and the usage defined in the licence determines how you can exploit that equity.

The three key elements of usage are:

Term: How the long the campaign will run
Territory: The markets in which the campaign will run
Media: The channels on which the campaign will run

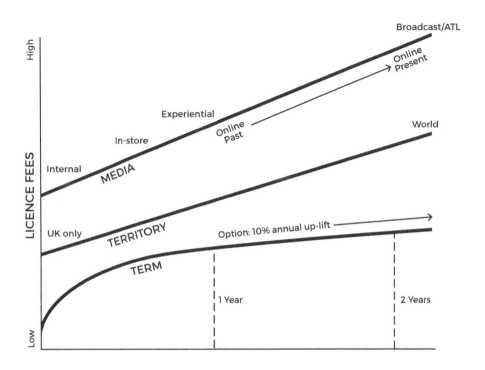

(i) Term

Historically, UK advertising campaign Terms were typically one year. Whilst music rights owners don't have set rate cards, they'd have a sense of the sync licence fee that a particular song or recording could command in their market for that period. Of course, they'd want brands to license for a full year rather than shorter periods and so would make short Terms disproportionately poor value. Here's a typical example:

Term	Example Fee	% of 1 Year Fee
12 months	£10,000	100%
6 months	£7,500	75%
3 months	£5,000	50%
1 month	£4,000	40%

In fact, some music rights owners may refuse to grant you a one or three month licence, especially for a famous music title. They want the big fees for the full year term.

Of course, media is now bought in fragmented bursts, especially for broadcast media. Your media agency might devise a plan which could be described as:

- **Six non-consecutive four week bursts within a twelve month window**

What does this mean to the Licensee and Licensor?

The brand (licensee) thinks:
"I'm only buying twenty-four weeks of media, which isn't even six months, so I expect a lower fee".

The music rights owner (licensor) thinks:
"This is essentially a full year licence – I don't care whether or not the campaign is on air the whole time – we'll charge them for a full year".

What's the take-out for marketers?

The music rights owners know they're unlikely to license the track you want to another brand in the gaps between your bursts. So there's no reason to grant a discount on what would have been the full year's fee. Yes, this seems unreasonable and quite contrary to how media is bought on your behalf by media agencies. However, the music industry is of a different mindset. They just think about the total length of the licence term, not the weight of media or how many people get to see your campaign. Music rights owners' perspective is that their title is tied up with your brand from the start of the first burst to the end of the last burst, irrespective of the breaks in between.

Let's now consider why the Term line on the graph is curved. This relates to Options which we'll examine in more detail in Section Three, Chapter 13. For now, remember that if you include an option to extend the Term by the same period again, it's usually possible to limit any fee increase to 10% above that which you paid in the initial term – provided that you exercise the option before the term expires. Here's how it works:

Term	Example Fee	% Uplift
Initial Term	£10,000	N/A
Second Term	£11,000	10% on initial term fee
Third Term	£12,100	10% on second term fee

You might think that you deserve a discount as a repeat customer if you extend the licence. In any other industry you might be right… but that's not how the music business works. What you should know is that if you don't include options in your original deal, the fee escalation for successive terms will be far greater than 10%. In other words, you are in a better position to negotiate what you might like to happen in the future while you are brokering the initial deal. Any bargaining power you may have will effectively be reduced to zero after the fact and you will certainly pay more.

(ii) Territory

Just as a reminder, when brands speak about "markets", music rights owners speak about "territories". So in any sync licence, the territory section lists the countries or markets in which the campaign is intended to run.

As you might expect, the more markets, the higher the fee. In the Usage graph at the start of this chapter you can see this clearly with a steep line from UK only on the left, to World on the right.

As a marketer, there are a few issues you need to understand about Territory:

(a) Bulk Buying vs. Targeted Buying
It's a common problem in decentralised businesses that the global marketing team doesn't have complete control over the local market teams. So the former doesn't know in advance what the latter needs. They simply can't predict which local markets will run the campaign until it's been produced and possibly tested locally.

When buying third-party IP rights, the "sledgehammer to crack a nut" solution is simply to buy a global licence. This will of course command a premium fee and could turn out to be very wasteful if only a handful of markets run the campaign.

Alternatively, the more cautious approach is to buy only the markets you need now, and negotiate options for all the others which have even the slightest chance of running the campaign. You must secure those options in advance to avoid excessive fee inflation arising from future re-negotiation. In contrast, the music rights owners will resist the grant of options. They may say, "Let's deal with that when the time comes," which should sound the alarm bells to keep negotiating. That said, if you subsequently exercise many options and end up buying most of the world piecemeal, you'll end up paying more than had you bought a global licence from the outset.

It's a tough call, but you need a clear perspective on which markets you need now and which ones you may need in future.

(b) "Don't See, Don't Care"
When brokering licences for US controlled music titles, or titles written or recorded by American talent, be aware of their perspective on "Domestic" versus "Foreign" markets.

For managers of US talent, America is the World and everywhere else is less significant. Yes, that's a bit harsh, but it's not so far from the truth in many cases. This is even more true when the talent is very successful in the States. If you can exclude the US from your campaign, it will dramatically lower the licence fees. Whilst artists and their managers will really care whether or not their domestic audience can see a campaign, they're less concerned if it's invisible on their home turf. For example, American actors sometimes appear in Japanese commercials, which no US consumer ever sees. The talent is happy to take the large fee, but the fans at home aren't aware of the TV spot. This concept is wonderfully demonstrated in the movie *Lost In Translation,* where Bob Harris (played by Bill Murray) features in the "Suntory Time!" campaign for Suntory Whisky. To some degree, this perspective is also true for music artists. Of course this has huge implications for online campaigns as we'll see in Section three, Chapter 11 on geo locking.

(c) *"They're famous here. So they're expensive everywhere"*
Perhaps contrary to (b) above is a US perspective which doesn't acknowledge that huge domestic success might not translate in foreign markets. I've worked on campaigns where our client wanted to license a track by an American artist who was very successful at home but unknown in Europe. Naturally the US option fees were very high, but so too were the European market fees. The artist's US label and management didn't care that the artist was unknown in Europe, their approach to global pricing was driven solely by a US perspective.

(iii) Media

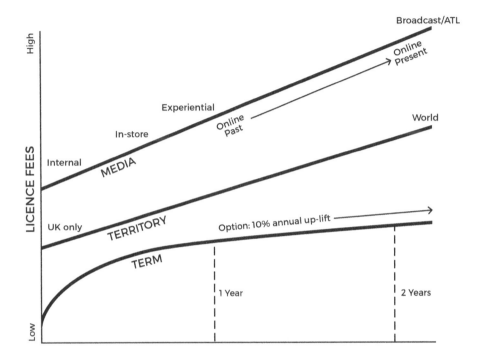

I've included the graph here again to demonstrate music rights owners' approach to pricing Media.

Media	Example Fee	% of TV
TV	£10,000	100%
Cinema	£6,500	65%
Radio	£3,500	35%

This wasn't set in stone, but the general trend was that TV attracted the top fees, Cinema was cheaper, with Radio cheaper still. Any other non-ATL usage was often referred to a "non-theatric" or "industrial" and considered to be less valuable to rights owners as the potential audience was smaller.

Of course the internet changed everything and online media was initially bundled into ATL campaigns with little impact on cost, particularly during the second half of the noughties. It was accepted that all online use would be global even if the ATL campaign was limited to local markets.

As a marketer, you need to be aware that this has all changed. From 2013 onwards, we've seen major music rights owners, especially music publishers, take a very aggressive stance on online pricing. It's no longer just bundled into ATL campaigns but is seen as a channel equally as valuable. This reflects how brands use online, especially those targeted at a young demographic who often shun TV in favour of YouTube. No longer can you think "it's just online, so the music will be cheap". If it's on YouTube, many music rights owners will consider that almost as valuable as bought broadcast TV media.

(iv) Context

(a) Content vs. Media

It's imperative to clearly list all the pieces of video content onto which you want to dub the music. If it's an ATL spot, there will probably be a broadcast version which will also run online. However, there may also be various other online-only videos which might include "behind the scenes", "the making of", "film of the film", "interviews", "out-takes" plus a long form version of the spot for in-store usage. These may contain elements of the main ATL spot but will probably also include additional footage. In the licence request you need to clearly list:

- **Each content piece**
- **The media / channels in which that particular piece will be used**

Don't just lump "behind the scenes", "the making of" into your media list for the ATL spot. They are not media channels but separate content pieces, hence the need to create a clear list so rights owners can see which piece of content is to be used in which media.

(b) Overt vs. Subtle Branding

Many marketers misunderstand how music rights owners think about the "context of use", especially for online video. It's important to be completely transparent about your intentions.

If the online video is overtly branded and product-led, it will appear to music rights owners as if it's a commercial. The fact that it's for online use only and not in ATL bought TV media is less significant – it's a piece of advertising and the licence fees charged will reflect that.

In contrast, if your online video is mostly educational, music rights owners will price it differently. Let's say your brand is a supermarket retailer. You might have a strand of your YouTube channel devoted to cooking and recipes. The products you sell might be subtly visible in the video, but essentially it's a "how to cook this dish" video. Music publishers and record labels won't view this as overt advertising and will be more lenient on licence fees. In contrast, the online usage of your blockbuster Christmas TV spot will be treated differently.

Remember that context of use is an important cost driver. You must be transparent about your intentions and disclose the full script of each film as part of the licence request. Sometimes rights owners may even ask to see the storyboard.

(v) "Buy-out"

This is a particular bug-bear of mine. Brands and agencies frequently use the term "buy-out" which suggests that they've bought out all rights in a particular piece of third-party IP. This often leads to the false assumption that the brand or agency has broad flexibility of use. Sadly, this is flawed thinking.

When discussing commercial catalogue music, the brand or agency haven't bought out the rights, they've just purchased a licence which will be limited by term, territory, media and context of use.

I recommend you don't use the term "buy-out". Instead, refer to a "licence".

Chapter summary

In this chapter we've examined how usage is a key driver in determining sync licence fees. We've learned that:

- **"Term" is the length of licence period**
- **Short terms are disproportionately expensive**
- **"Territory" covers the markets in which the campaign runs**
- **The larger the Territory, the higher the fees, especially if it includes USA**
- **"Media" covers the on and off line channels in which the campaign runs**
- **Online media is increasingly priced like broadcast media**
- **Context of use is also an important cost driver**
- **The more overt the branding, the higher the licence fee**

Reader's notes

(i) Big Mental Note

(ii) One Big Step

CHAPTER 10
Most favoured nations

In this chapter we'll explore the frequently misunderstood term Most Favoured Nations by which multiple music rights owners ensure they receive the same fees.

To badly paraphrase Churchill…

"Never in the field of music licensing has one term been used by so many yet understood by so few".

(i) What it really means

Most Favoured Nations, or "MFN", is a key provision that marketers need to understand. It's an upwards-only price equalisation device. MFN is very common in music licensing even though it's essentially anti-competitive.

Many sync licensing staff at record labels and music publishers have terms and conditions in their email signatures along these lines:

All quotes are provided on an MFN basis unless specified otherwise.
Quotes provided are strictly subject to approval.
Approvals given are strictly subject to a signed contract.

To understand the most common usage of MFN between record labels and music publishers, we need a quick recap of master and publishing rights.

We've previously learned that there are two fundamentally separate rights in commercial catalogue music:

	Song	Recording
Known as	Publishing Rights	Master Rights
Usually controlled by	Music Publisher	Record Label

In a sync licence deal where you want to use an existing recording of a song, you'll have a minimum of two deals to negotiate:

- **One with the music publisher for the song**
- **One with the record label for the sound recording**

You might make an offer to each rights owner for the title you want to use, or you might ask them to quote. At this point, it's important to understand that many of the sync licensing executives in the UK major music labels and publishers (and the larger independents) know each other. In fact they quite regularly swap jobs in the annual merry-go-round of sync licensing positions. It's a relatively small community of less than fifty key players.

When asking for a quote from the label and publisher of a specific music title, the two relevant sync licensing executives you approach may liaise with one another to ensure their quotes match. Yes of course that's price fixing, but it happens. In some cases, corporate governance has banned this practice so the sync executives get round that by using the MFN device.

It's important to understand the perspective of the record label and music publisher on pricing which explains the prevalence of MFN. Each one thinks:

"Why should we receive any less than the other side?"

How does MFN work in practice?

The music publisher might quote:
£10,000 MFN with master

The record label might quote:
£10,000 MFN with publishing

However, let's say that the publisher and label quoted differently like this:

The music publisher might quote:
£15,000 MFN with master

The record label might quote:
£10,000 MFN with publishing

Unless you manage to convince the publisher to lower their fee to match the record label, then the label's fee rises to match the publisher's. <u>MFN only works upwards</u>.

Where there's just one publisher and one label, the outcome looks like this:

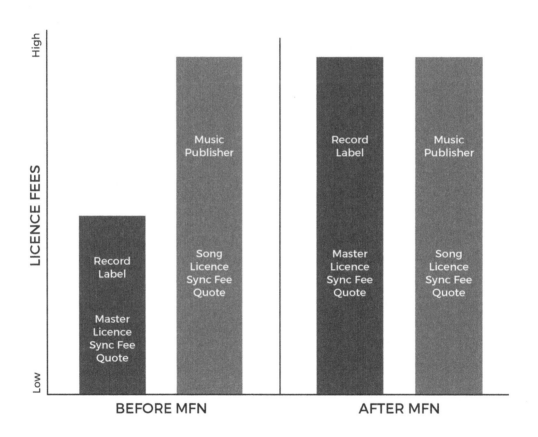

However, very often one song can be controlled by multiple music publishers. This usually occurs where there are two or more songwriters each of whom have a different music publisher. A song with two publishers isn't necessarily split 50/50 between them – it all depends on the creative input of each songwriter. It could be 60/40, 70/30, 80/20, 90/10 or any other multitude of splits. Where there's an unequal share, the "majority publisher" with the biggest share will usually call the shots on fees. Confusingly, it's customary for multiple music publishers to quote *based on a 100% share* even though they don't control 100%. In the jargon, multiple publishers are called "co-publishers", often referred to in quotes as "co-pubs".

Let's assume the music track you want has one record label and two music publishers. You ask them all to quote, they don't liaise and respond with different quotes:

Music publisher 1
£11,000 100% share – MFN with co-pub & master

Music publisher 2
£15,000 100% share – MFN with co-pub & master

Record label
£10,000 MFN with publishing

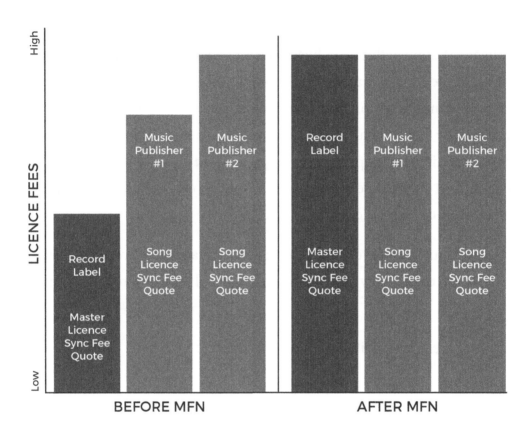

As you can see above, if all parties refuse to negotiate on fees or *remove the MFN provision*, the fees rise to the level of the highest quote, in this case £15,000.

Let's assume the song is controlled 50/50 between the two co-publishers, then the final outcome will be:

Music publisher 1

£15,000 100% share – MFN with co-pub & master

(of which publisher 1 receives £7,500 for their 50% share of the song)

Music publisher 2

£15,000 100% share – MFN with co-pub & master

(of which publisher 2 receives £7,500 for their 50% share of the song)

Record label

£15,000 MFN with publishing

(ii) Can MFN be broken?

Remember what we said before about the perspective of the record label and music publisher on pricing. Each one thinks:

"Why should we receive any less than the other side?"

By now you'll be thinking, "Why can't we just ask the record labels and music publishers to stop using MFN?" It's a valid question though MFN is such an established practice in the sync licensing business, it is very rarely waived. Here are a few observations:

When might it be possible to waive MFN?

Where the song has been recorded ("covered") by a different artist from the person who wrote it, some record labels will agree to remove "MFN with publishing" if the stature of the song is much higher than that of the cover artist.

When is it never possible to waive MFN?

- **Where the songwriter(s) and artist is the same person/people on the track you want, the music publisher and record label will always insist on MFN between publishing and master rights.**
- **Where the song has multiple publishers, they will always insist on MFN between co-publishers.**

Key watch out for marketers:

MFN provisions are complex and can seriously damage your music budget. It's an area where external expert support can help avoid expensive problems. If you do decide to go it alone, ensure you've identified all the rights owners involved in the track you want. Next, secure quotes (or approval of offers) from each and every one. Examine the small print carefully and email signatures for references to MFN. In fact even if it's not in the quote, MFN will probably be a provision in the long form licence.

Chapter summary

In this chapter we've discovered that Most Favoured Nations is a very common device used by music rights owners to equalise sync licence fees. We've learned that MFN:

- **is a form of anti-competitive price fixing**
- **is an upwards only device**
- **equalises fees paid to a music publisher and record label on the same deal**
- **equalises pro-rata fees paid to co-publishers on the same deal**
- **may be a contractual requirement even if not mentioned at quote stage**
- **is very common in the sync licensing industry**
- **is rarely waived except for "cover" recordings by emerging artists of famous songs or songs written by successful songwriters**

Reader's notes

(i) Big Mental Note

(ii) One Big Step

CHAPTER 11
Geo locking

In this chapter we'll examine how music rights owners have changed their approach to the licensing of Territory for online usage. Many are now insisting on geo locking also called geo blocking.

In Chapter 9 we looked at the Territory element of Usage and in particular the attitude of US rights owners to the use of their music overseas. This perspective finds form within online media through the growing demand by music rights owners for geo locking, also called geo blocking.

(i) The benefits of invisibility

During the second half of the noughties and first few years of the 2010s, music rights owners would generally tolerate global online usage as part of a single market broadcast media sync licence. For example, whether your brand was targeted only at UK consumers or had an international market, if your specific campaign was aimed at the UK through bought TV media, it was accepted that the film could be globally accessible via brand and agency sites; plus social media as its influence grew.

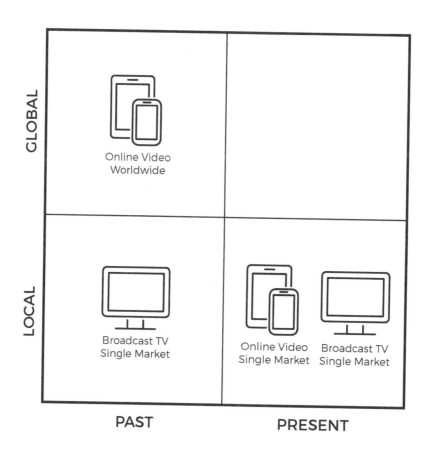

From around 2013, this started to change along with the very aggressive licence fee increases for online usage. Currently, we're seeing major rights owners, especially music publishers, demand that the online element of campaigns be restricted to the same markets as the offline element. It's not uncommon to see quotes for a UK only TV campaign dictate that online usage is also restricted to the same market. This tallies with the growing perception by the music industry that online, primarily YouTube, is as effective as TV and hence needs to be licensed at the same or similar sync fees.

If your online campaign can be restricted to specific markets, there are clear benefits to being invisible elsewhere.

(ii) Impact on price

The primary benefit is licence fee price. Of course a global TV sync licence fee will be very significantly higher than one just for the UK. Here's a typical proportional breakdown:

Territory	Example Fee	% of World
World	£100,000	100%
USA	£50,000	50%
UK	£20,000	20%

We are now seeing the same effect for online fees – whether this is earned, owned or paid-for. If you can't restrict online use to a single market, you may pay a significant multiple for global use.

(iii) Implementation

If your video is only uploaded to YouTube, you can geo lock access to it through the YouTube Partner programme. The brand's YouTube channel must become a YouTube Partner for this to happen, and if implemented, the key watch outs are:

- **YouTube should be the only location where the video is hosted**
- **Don't upload the video to your own corporate site**
- **Mandate that agency partners and their supply chain cannot upload the video to their own site or channels**
- **All vendors, partners and media can only embed a link to your YouTube channel on their own sites. They cannot host the video on their own sites.**

This will seem draconian to your agencies, partners and media. However, it's the only safe method to ensure that you don't breach the terms of a sync licence in which online usage is geo locked to a specific market.

Chapter summary

In this chapter we've discovered that the need to geo lock online content is becoming commonplace for many brand campaigns.

We've learned that some music rights owners:

- **no longer grant global online licences where the offline element isn't global**
- **insist that the online element is geo locked to match offline**

We've also learned that successful geo locking necessitates:

- **uploading videos to a single location i.e. YouTube**
- **the YouTube channel must be in the name of a "YouTube Partner"**
- **visibility on third-party sites must be via embedded YouTube links**

Reader's notes

(i) Big Mental Note

(ii) One Big Step

CHAPTER 12
Time and competition

In this chapter we'll examine two key licence fee cost drivers that many brands and ad agencies fail to control: urgency and competitive landscape.

(i) Urgency

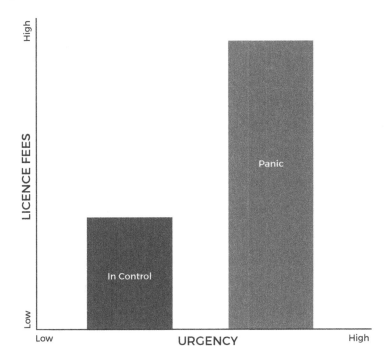

As we saw in Section Three Chapter 6, approval chains can be long. So you need to allow lots of time when brokering sync licence deals as clearances don't happen in a day or even just a few days. It can take a week or sometimes much longer.

When brands, or more usually their agencies, leave music to the last minute, the licence request to music right owners becomes urgent. Indeed, music publishers and record labels are continually amazed that brands and agencies appear to exist in a constant state of panic – everything is urgent. How do they respond? With significant fee inflation. Where there is panic, there are high licence fees as rights owners know that the brand and its agency are backed against the wall and have little or no time to find alternative music tracks. Give yourself more time, and your ability to negotiate improves.

(ii) Competitive landscape : Hero tracks & back-ups

Closely linked to urgency is competitive landscape. All too often, brands become fixated on one music track which is often the one that was dubbed by the agency to the mood film during creative development. Everyone on both the brand and agency teams falls in love with this track – and this position becomes further entrenched if the music scores highly during research. What so frequently happens is that no-one thinks to check if the music track can actually be cleared, and if so, at what price. When approaches to the rights owners are finally made, late in the production schedule, if the resulting quote is very high, there's a tendency for the brand to concede and pay the quoted fee. There's a sense that "we have nowhere else to go" because everyone's so emotionally attached to the particular music track.

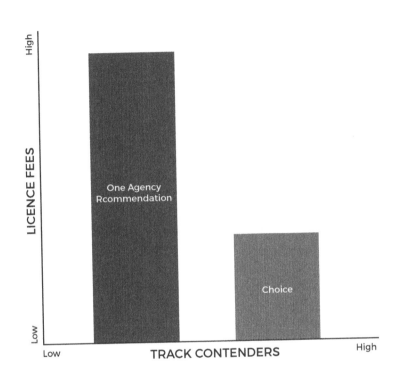

The root of this problem is the "single agency recommendation". A tendency for creative agencies to present the "one and only" music track that works with their creative idea and a refusal to accept that any other can perform the same function. The viewpoint often becomes entrenched if the brand, or its procurement team, pushes back citing cost as a reason.

To avoid this problem, from the very outset, ensure that:

- **Your creative agency presents multiple music track ideas, even for the mood film**
- **You check the clearability and cost of all music track contenders**
- **You assess both creative and commercial attributes of each track before becoming attached to any one title**

Chapter summary

In this chapter we've highlighted the flaws in the ad agency practice of a single recommend track whose clearance isn't addressed until the eleventh hour.

We've learned that urgency:

- **empowers music rights owners**
- **can irritate approval parties, making them less cooperative**
- **creates disproportionately high fee inflation**

We've learned that that single track recommendations mean:

- **no "walk away" position for the brand**
- **little or no bargaining power for the brand**
- **disproportionately high fee inflation**

The above points reinforce the widely used "Cheap, Quick, Good" model below in which customers usually want all three attributes but suppliers will only ever grant two.

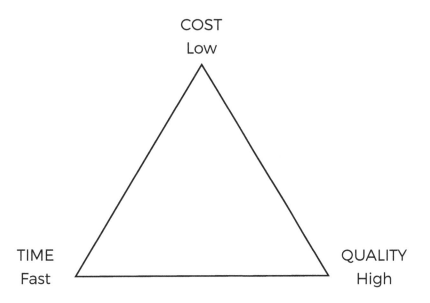

Reader's notes

(i) Big Mental Note

(ii) One Big Step

CHAPTER 13
Licence options

In this chapter we'll examine a powerful device for controlling future licence fee inflation: licence options. When successfully employed, options can pre-determine licence fees for future extensions to Term, Territory, Media or Context.

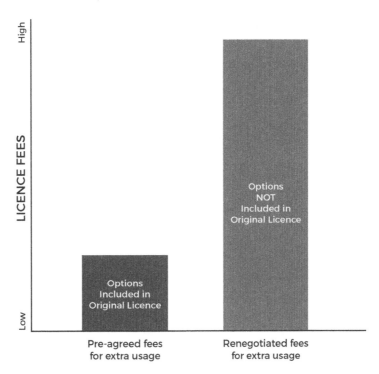

(i) The benefits of covering all bases

The successful inclusion of Options in sync licences allows you to future-proof commercial terms to cover campaign elements you may need but aren't yet committed to. The benefit of Options for brands is that:

- **It commits the rights owner to "sell" you a licence extension at a specific price**
- **It doesn't commit you to "buy" that extension unless you exercise the option**

What is an option?
It's a commitment by the music rights owner to extend the licence by term, territory, media or context of use within specific constraints for a specific fee.

How does the brand exercise the option?

Usually by a simple written instruction together with a purchase order ("PO") for the relevant licence fee which must be paid before the Option period starts.

Why don't all licences include options?

- **Music rights owners don't want to grant options. They want you to renegotiate from a position of weakness which allow rights owners to substantially increase fees.**
- **Agencies want the work of renegotiation, as extra hours on the time sheet justifies their fees.**
- **Unless you negotiate options up-front, your sync licences won't include them.**

How do you know which options to ask for and how to negotiate them? This is a complex task for which you may need external expert support.

Chapter summary

In this chapter we've examined the powerful device of licence options and the benefits to brands who successfully employ them.

We've learned that licence options:

- **can cover extensions to Term, Territory, Media or Context**
- **can predetermine future fees and avoid renegotiation from a weak position**
- **must be negotiated up-front and aren't routinely granted**
- **favour the licensee so are reluctantly granted by the licensor**
- **are a powerful tool to control fee inflation**
- **necessitate smart up-front media planning**

Reader's notes

(i) Big Mental Note

(ii) One Big Step

SECTION FOUR

What happens when things go wrong? The risks and how to mitigate them

We've learned how music rights work and how to buy them efficiently. However, an off-the-record chat with many marketers reveals an array of horror stories relating to music deals. Being held to ransom at the eleventh hour; cease and desist letters; unexpected penalty fees and even legal proceedings. These are some of the risks confronting marketers and agencies who are unfamiliar with music licensing. In this section we'll unpick those risks so you can fully understand where the pitfalls lie. More importantly, you'll learn how to successfully manage those risks.

CHAPTER 14
Unauthorised use

In this chapter we'll examine the risks for brands who use music without valid licences in place.

Without getting too bogged down in legalese, as a marketer you should understand two main types of unauthorised music usage:

- **Copyright infringement**
- **Breach of licence**

We'll look at each in turn and the strategies to avoid them.

(i) Copyright infringement

With the sole exception of proven public domain works, if you use music in a brand marketing campaign, you need a licence in both composition and sound recording. Period. There are no ifs or buts. No excuses. Claiming that you didn't know won't protect you. Likewise, it's not sufficient to say you couldn't find the rights owners.

Without a valid licence, you are guilty of copyright infringement. You are breaking the law and complicit in illegal activity, whether or not this was intentional.

Yes, I appreciate that seems a bit melodramatic, but it's highlighted for a reason. I've personally witnessed brands and agencies discussing the pros and cons of "trying to get away with it". Highly educated, intelligent professionals considering the risks of getting caught for intentional theft of intellectual property.

Broadly speaking, in the marketing and advertising worlds, copyright infringement is the use of an existing composition and/or sound recording within a campaign without a valid licence. Such usage can infringe copyright controlled by music publishers and/or record labels.

Thankfully, most marketers and agencies know not to intentionally dub unlicensed music on a campaign film and hope that no-one will notice. So intentional unlicensed use is less common now than in the past. However, I still see examples of unintentional unlicensed use, usually arising from misunderstandings between brand, multiple agencies and/or multiple music supervisors, all assuming that someone else has secured the necessary licences.

Whether the unlicensed use was intentional or not, the music rights owners involved are perfectly entitled to make a legal claim and in some cases do; especially when the songwriters or artists concerned would have denied the licence request had it been properly submitted. The usual outcome is that the music rights owners approach the infringing party and demand:

- **the temporary suspension of the campaign**
- **a retrospective licence**
- **a market rate sync licence fee for the required usage**

- **an additional penalty fee, e.g. 50%, 100% or 200% of the market rate fee**
- **A public apology**

In simple terms, the solution to unauthorised usage is to ensure you have licences in place which are fully aligned with your media plan i.e. the usage you need should be accurately reflected in the licence that grants permission for that usage.

(ii) Breach of licence

Breach of Licence is slightly less serious than Copyright Infringement in that it assumes you've already secured permission for the usage but have gone beyond the agreed restrictions. However, the rights owners, artist and songwriters may still be offended and wish to make a legal claim.

Breach of licence is fairly common and occurs when the licensed music is used as follows:

- **On the licensed film beyond the expiry of the licensed term**
- **On the licensed film beyond the licensed territories**
- **On the licensed film beyond the licensed media**
- **On the licensed film but with unauthorised edits, durations, adaptions or versions**
- **On other films**

I most commonly see these problems when licences are brokered on behalf of a centralised global marketing team, initially responding to requests from their colleagues in local markets. However, the local markets subsequently proceed with new or altered usage without first checking with their global colleagues if that's covered in the licences.

This is a common problem across multi-market brands, especially when local markets have a high degree of autonomy. When it occurs, one of several things can happen:

- **The global marketing team discover the unlicensed usage, demand that their local market colleagues terminate the usage temporarily and negotiate a reasonable retrospective licence fee before allowing the campaign to continue.**
- **The global marketing team discover the unlicensed usage, admit the error to the music rights owners and negotiate an expensive though acceptable retrospective licence fee to allow the campaign to continue uninterrupted.**
- **The global marketing team discover the unlicensed usage, demand that their local market colleagues terminate the usage immediately and hope that the music rights owners never find out.**
- **The global marketing team discover the unlicensed usage, they ignore it and allow it to continue, hoping that the music rights owners never find out.**
- **The global marketing team discover the unlicensed usage, they ignore it and allow it to continue. The music rights owners discover it, issue a cease and desist letter, demand the campaign is immediately halted, claim for both a high retrospective licence fee and unreasonably high penalty fee.**

Of course, the first option is the recommended course of action. Generally, if you "put your hand up" and admit the error, having temporarily halted the campaign, you'll find that music rights owners will be reasonable in their response. In contrast, if you knowingly allow an unauthorised usage to continue and are then "found out", expect no mercy from the music rights owners.

Chapter summary

In this chapter we've discussed the risk for brands that use music without valid licences in place. We've examined strategies to mitigate that risk.

We've learned that:

- **There's no excuse for deliberate unlicensed usage by a brand**
- **Brands should expect legal claims and penalty fees for unlicensed use**
- **Music rights owners can be litigious. They fiercely protect their copyrights**
- **A policy of honesty and transparency is always best**
- **Rights owners are usually more lenient to brands who admit their mistakes**
- **It's wise to suspend an unlicensed campaign then negotiate required usage**
- **It's always cheaper to secure a valid licence upfront before usage begins**

Reader's notes

(i) Big Mental Note

(ii) One Big Step

CHAPTER 15
Sound-a-likes / Passing off

In this chapter we'll examine two specific areas where brands and agencies frequently encounter legal problems with music rights owners: sound-a-likes and passing off. We'll look at the temptations that drive these creative routes plus their financial and legal consequences.

We've learned about unauthorised usage in the form of:

- **Copyright Infringement**
- **Breach of Licence**

Sadly it doesn't end there as brands, and especially their agencies, sometimes adopt other questionable practices which get them into hot water with music rights owners. These take the form of:

- **Sound-a-likes**
- **Passing off**

(a) Sound-a-likes

Sound-a-like is an often used and abused term but my own definition is:

"The briefing of a composer to create a supposedly new composition that's intentionally similar to another existing work, especially when that work has been denied for use in an advertising campaign or been quoted by the rights owner(s) at an unaffordable level."

Of course you're thinking: *"We'd never do that... and nor would our agency."*

However, you only need to watch commercial TV for a few evenings to hear how prevalent the practice is. You hear the opening bar of music on a TV spot and it sounds strangely familiar, yet once it gets started it's not the song you thought it was. In some cases you can even name the song. Right now I'm thinking of a TV spot for a mobile phone retailer which uses a track that's very similar to an iconic song by Australia's most famous hard rock band. Frankly I'm surprised they got away with it (though maybe there's a lawsuit rumbling behind the scenes).

So, let's look at how Sound-a-likes happen:

- **Agency recommends existing song to brand during creative development**
- **Brand loves it**
- **Song scores highly with focus groups during script research**
- **Song is dubbed to animatic**
- **Song continues to remain the clear favourite during production**
- **By post production agency thinks, "we better check it's clearable"**
- **Song is quoted far outside available budget (or denied)**

- **Everyone panics**
- **Agency pleads with music rights owners to lower price**
- **Music rights owners refuse**
- **Everyone panics even more**
- **Agency commissions desperate search for alternative tracks**
- **No other tracks measure up to the favourite song**
- **There are only five days until the delivery deadline of the TV spot**
- **Agency commissions composer to "create something similar"**
- **Agency specifically references the song they really wanted in the brief**
- **Composer delivers "something similar"**
- **Campaign launches**
- **Music publisher of favourite song sends Cease and Desist letter to brand's CEO claiming copyright infringement**

I have personally seen this happen several times despite my intervention, advising the agency concerned not to pursue this path. The uncomfortable truth is that brands and especially agencies have a resolutely optimistic mind-set which manifests itself in a "nothing is impossible" mantra. A refusal to admit defeat – a denial of "No means No". Whilst this can be very empowering in overcoming some hurdles, it's extremely dangerous when dealing with music rights owners.

What does this mean for marketers?

Sound-a-likes are another form of copyright infringement and in my view it's unacceptable behaviour by a brand or agency. If you can't get permission to use the track you want (or can't afford it), find another track, don't attempt to copy it. If you still pursue this path and are confronted with a legal claim from the music publisher of the work you've copied, sadly you deserve it. I know that sounds harsh and pedantic, but it's meant to.

It's offensive to music publishers when brands and agencies try to copy their work. It's of even greater offence to the songwriters concerned especially if they denied the original request. The resulting legal claims are therefore swift and severe.

As a marketer, mandate that your agency cannot commission sound-a-likes and if they still insist on doing so, ensure that they fully indemnify the brand against any and all subsequent legal claims by third parties.

What are the watch outs?

(i) Musicologists
The Merriam-Webster Dictionary defines musicology as:

"The study of music as a branch of knowledge or field of research as distinct from composition or performance". So the person who studies musicology is a musicologist.

In the UK, there are a small handful of musicologists who advise advertising agencies, especially on bespoke compositions and the risks associated with them. These musicologists have extensive court experience as expert witnesses and therefore a sense of how a claim may play out if it isn't settled before court.

A musicologist might advise an agency how their chosen composer should amend the first draft sound-a-like composition. e.g. "The work should still be reminiscent of the denied or out-priced favourite song, but not so close as to risk a legal claim from the music publisher concerned". The agency instructs the composer to make the changes, the musicologist approves them, and everyone breathes a sigh of relief.

However, the musicologist will indemnify neither the brand nor the agency if there's a legal claim. All they've done is give their expert opinion but it's not an insurance policy. If the case proceeds to court where the intent to copy is exposed in the commissioning brief, the musicologist's advice won't protect you.

(ii) The urban myth of six notes
I've sat in meetings with advertising agency executives who've said something along the lines of:

"… but we've only got the first six notes the same and after that it's different – so that's OK, right?"

Whether it's four, six, eight or ten notes, any urban myth about what's OK and what's not is exactly that – a myth.

(iii) The Composer's contract indemnifies us
Composer commissioning agreements should include:

- **A warranty that states the work is wholly original and doesn't infringe the rights of any third parties**

- **A full and unlimited indemnity to cover any breach of that warranty by the composer**

In the event of a legal claim, you might think that you can stand behind the composer as they'll be the party that gets sued. However, composers tend not to have deep pockets, unless they're scoring Hollywood movies. Typically legal claims are directed at the brand and the agency.

The outcome of all this is:
Do not ever be tempted to commission sound-a-likes. The risks are just too great.

(b) Passing off

There are various legal definitions of "passing off" but in the music licensing sphere I define it as follows:

The deliberate attempt to create a re-record of a properly licensed song or composition where the new recording is similar or identical to an existing original artist recording and so causes confusion in the mind of the listener.

Re-records are very common in UK advertising. Provided that you've secured the necessary synchronisation licence for the song or composition from the music publisher, you're free to make a new recording of it. Of course the synchronisation licence request needs to disclose that you plan to make a re-record. In many cases the music publisher may demand to hear the re-record and share it with the original songwriter(s) before full approval is granted for this treatment of the song.

The key benefits of re-records are:

- **You only need a synchronisation licence in the song or composition**
- **You do not need to license an existing original artist master recording (though of course you do need to cover any and all costs in creating the re-record).**

However, you cannot simply create a new re-record that intentionally sounds like an existing artist recording – to do so is known as "passing off" and may lead to legal claims from the artist who feels they've been misrepresented and their record label who feels you've deliberately avoided paying a licence fee for their recording.

To avoid this risk, I have some simple tips that should be included in any written brief to a music production company or arranger/producer who've been commissioned to create the re-record. The intention is that the re-record must be *noticeably different* from the original artist recording.

- **Singer gender – If the original singer is male, use a female session singer**
- **Instrumentation / Arrangement – Make it different from the original recording**
- **Musical Key – Make it different from the original recording**
- **Tempo – Make it different from the original recording**

Make sure all these instructions to the supplier are in writing. There needs to be evidence that you actively briefed the supplier to avoid creating a re-record that passes off as the original artist recording.

Chapter summary

In this chapter we've discussed the risk for brands who commission sound-a-likes or re-records that "pass-off" as the original artist recording.

On sound-a-likes, we've learned that:

- It's tempting to copy songs whose licence fees exceed the available budget
- It's tempting to copy songs where clearance has been denied
- Songwriters find sound-a-likes particularly offensive
- Music publishers are increasingly litigious in response to sound-a-likes
- Musicologists can advise but won't offer indemnities
- Changing a few notes won't mask an intent to copy
- Commissioning sound-a-likes is a high risk strategy
- It's safer to find an alternative song that conveys the same emotion

On "passing off", we've learned that:

- "Passing off" is typically relevant to re-records
- It's tempting to copy original artist recordings to avoid a master licence fee
- Artists find passing-off particularly offensive
- Record labels can be litigious about passing off, especially in the USA
- Musicologists can advise but won't offer indemnities
- It's safer to create an entirely original arrangement of the licensed song

Reader's notes

(i) Big Mental Note

(ii) One Big Step

CHAPTER 16
Who's going to know?

*In this chapter we'll explore how a consumer-style perspective
on uploading videos is highly problematic when adopted by
brand marketers and agencies.*

In our personal lives, we've become accustomed to uploading content on a daily basis to our personal social media channels. Everything from selfies to pet videos to our every waking thought. Generally the younger the person, the more they share – hence the stigma of "generation overshare". There's a sense that this content can live forever on our channels – our digital self becomes immortal – sometimes the person we want to be rather than who we really are.

This mind set can become dangerous when members of "generation overshare" have roles as brand marketers and advertising executives. I've witnessed the above attitude to uploading brand marketing content videos – a sense that, ".. because it's just on YouTube and it's not a commercial, it's insignificant. So we don't really need to clear music rights and the film can stay up on YouTube forever".

This stance is wholly wrong and effectively condones unauthorised usage which constitutes infringement of copyright.

It's certainly the case that in the late noughties, many brands posted content with unlicensed music which wasn't identified by music rights owners. The music publishers and record labels either weren't aware this was happening or didn't yet have the tools to track it.

This situation has changed and music rights owners now see unauthorised use by brands as a real cash cow; a golden opportunity to charge high penalty fees from a position of strength, given the alternative is to sue for damages.

Rights owner vigilance

Music publishers and record labels use software to detect unlicensed online usage of their music. In some cases, unlicensed video content will suffer an automatic take-down. Elsewhere there may be human intervention whereby the rights owner contacts the brand or agency (the licensee) to make amends and pay the appropriate licence fees. Even for properly licensed online uses, rights owners routinely check if the video has been taken down by the licensee when the licence expires. Where this doesn't happen, some rights owners will contact the licensee to offer a chance to renew the licence – though the window within which to do this will be short.

Fees for unlicensed usage or extensions to licences are increasingly a key part of rights owners' sync income.

Chapter summary

In this chapter we've learned that:

- Brands can't upload videos "with abandon" in the manner of consumers
- Music in brand online campaigns must be properly licensed
- Online usage is limited by Term which will almost never be in perpetuity
- Music rights owners pro-actively seek unlicensed usage by brands
- Unlicensed usage is punished by take-downs and penalty licence fees

Reader's notes

(i) Big Mental Note

(ii) One Big Step

CHAPTER 17
"What's the worst that can happen?"

In this chapter we'll examine the legal, financial and practical consequences of unlicensed music usage

So much of this book is drawn from real life experiences where I've witnessed problems created by marketers and their agencies which could have easily been avoided. Where there's little respect for third-party IP, there can be a mind set of "don't ask for permission, ask for forgiveness".

This attitude will result in trouble and pain for the brand or agency as music rights owners generally don't forgive deliberate unauthorised use. Instead, the likely outcomes are:

- **Cease and desist letters**
- **Penalty fees**
- **Injunctions**
- **Content take downs**
- **Channel take downs**

Let's look at these in turn:

(i) Cease and desist letters

These are more widely used in the US than the UK, but nevertheless sometimes the first response by a rights owner will be a formal letter from their legal and business affairs team. Essentially, "stop the campaign immediately, then we'll discuss fees".

This is especially worrying for a campaign where any bought media is involved as clearly that investment will be wasted. Whilst brands should of course take legal advice on receipt of a cease and desist letter, ignoring it is not an option.

(ii) Penalty fees

Given the UK tends to be less litigious than the US, the usual first response to unauthorised usage will be an email or phone call which notifies the brand or agency that the rights owners are aware of the unlicensed campaign.

In most cases, the music rights owners will demand that the campaign temporarily stops while a deal can be worked out for the usage required – that's of course assuming that the artist and songwriters concerned don't deny the usage. It's essential that the brand complies with this demand – so you can then negotiate a deal in the absence of ongoing unauthorised usage.

While the campaign is paused, the music rights owners will want full disclosure of:

(a) The usage that has taken place so far

(b) The usage required for the future

Even if (a) is very short, say a few days or weeks, the music rights owner will set a licence fee comprising:

- **The basic fee had the brand sought advance permission for the initial use**
- **An additional penalty fee to compensate the failure to seek consent in advance**

The penalty fee is likely to be a percentage of the basic fee – This could be anything from 50% to 500%, but 50% to 100% is most common.

My advice here is: just pay the (a) fee that's demanded. You're not in a position to negotiate and if you're looking to continue the campaign, the focus should be on the (b) fee.

For (b), you are in a position, albeit weak, to negotiate as this usage hasn't yet happened. Your leverage is your ability to change the music track meaning the music rights owners of the unlicensed track would receive nothing for the future usage. It's seriously worth considering this option, and perhaps even dubbing an alternative track to the film, and sharing this with the rights owners of the track you initially used – this would support your argument that you could quite easily replace their track if they don't quote a reasonable fee for the future usage.

(iii) Injunctions

Your legal team can offer the best advice here, but it's rare in the UK that music rights owners injunct campaigns containing unlicensed music. In theory they could, so this can have huge financial implications for a major bought media campaign.

(iv) Content take downs

This video is no longer available
due to a copyright claim.
Sorry about that.

You may have seen the above message when searching for a video on YouTube. This happens following a "take down" of a video.

What you might not know is that music rights owners can apply the "take down" themselves – they don't even have to ask YouTube / Google.

So if you've invested many tens or even hundreds of thousands of pounds in the production of a glossy film but haven't cleared the music properly, your consumers will see the above screen fairly shortly after you post it to YouTube.

If the music right owners are feeling benevolent, they might warn you of the impending take down and ask that you remove the offending content first – but they are not obliged to do this. Your film can just disappear if the rights owners so wish.

(v) Channel take downs

This video is no longer available because the YouTube account associated with this video has been terminated due to multiple third-party notifications of copyright infringement.
Sorry about that.

If you post content with unlicensed music to YouTube, it's preferable for the rights owners to warn you about an impending take down, so you can remove it before they do.

Why is this?

Each take down counts as a "strike"… and YouTube has a "three strikes rule".

If there are three strikes against your YouTube channel, the entire channel is suspended.

Viewers seeking any content on your site will be met with the above message. Most brands would consider this very damaging to their reputation with consumers.

Chapter summary

In this chapter we've learned that:

- **Music rights owners will take swift action if they identify unlicensed usage**
- **Action may include legal claims, penalty fees and injunctions**
- **Penalty fees may be multiples of the regular licence fee**
- **Unlicensed YouTube videos suffer "take downs" resulting in one "strike"**
- **Three "strikes" results in suspension of the entire YouTube channel**

Reader's notes

(i) Big Mental Note

(ii) One Big Step

CHAPTER 18
Reputational damage

In this chapter we'll examine how unlicensed music usage can damage a brand beyond legal, financial and practical consequences.

You may know this quote:

> *"It takes 20 years to build a reputation and five minutes to ruin it.*
> *If you think about that, you'll do things differently."*
> WARREN BUFFETT

One of the most high profile UK illustrations of this thought was Gerald Ratner's infamous comment about the product lines of his eponymous jewellery chain:

> *"We also do cut-glass sherry decanters complete with six glasses on a silver-plated tray*
> *that your butler can serve you drinks on, all for £4.95. People say, 'How can you sell*
> *this for such a low price?' I say, because it's total crap."*
> GERALD RATNER, 1991.

This comment purportedly wiped £500 million from the value of Ratner's company.

Most recently, publicity surrounding the installation of software in VW diesel-engine cars that affected emissions testing has arguably caused significant damage to the brand's reputation. This lead to the departure of senior executives and legal action against the company. The effect on sales and the company's standing in the minds of potential car buyers may be profound.

What does this mean for marketers?

Consumers are vocal. The prevalent "have your say" sense of entitlement leads the public to believe that the world wants to hear their opinion about everything including brands. Whilst as professionals we may not like this, it's a reality that applies to the slightest transgression by brands, whether real or perceived.

In instances of unlicensed music usage, it's not uncommon for the artists affected to use social media to berate the offending brand. This is often quickly amplified by their fans and so within hours the alleged offence may become a consumer media news story. Irrespective of the facts, the artist's fans will almost certainly side with their idols and it's likely that populist consumer media will follow suit. What follows can be a vitriolic consumer outburst and demands for a boycott of the offending brand's goods or services. Of course this might blow over quickly, but it's still highly undesirable. In contrast, there might be more balanced comment in the broadsheets or trade press on the precise legal position but many consumers won't care about that. They're drawn to the drama of their favourite artist being wronged by an evil corporation. It's a classic David and Goliath story.

I've seen many examples where brands have been publicly castigated for perceived injustices against music artists. In some cases this was valid but in others not entirely so. The fact remains that the public, especially music fans, will almost always side with the artist and against corporations, irrespective of the facts. "Perception is reality" and how the brand is perceived to have behaved is what matters.

A recent development that empowers consumers to name and shame brands is the release of the .sucks domain. At the time of writing, URLs with this domain may be available to the public at a fraction of the price that brands might wish to pay in a defensive move. It's another example of "people power" that can be unleashed should brands be perceived to be stepping out of line.

Chapter summary

In this chapter we've learned that:

- **Unlicensed usage isn't just about legal and financial risk**
- **It's also about reputational risk**
- **Arguably a brand's reputation and good will is one of its greatest assets**

Reader's notes

(i) Big Mental Note

(ii) One Big Step

CHAPTER 19
Aligning media schedules with licences

In this chapter we'll explore how the alignment of media schedules with licence terms is central to successful music rights buying. The failure to achieve alignment is the root cause of many rights licensing problems.

In Section Four, Chapter 14 we looked at how unlicensed usage occurs when the manner in which you've used the music doesn't match the rights you've licensed. In other words, the campaign media schedule isn't aligned with the music licences.

This is a widespread problem for marketers because their media agencies:

- **Seek to maximise efficiency of media spend**
- **Will seize last minute media opportunities if they believe it serves their client**
- **Aren't concerned about usage rights of third-party IP within client campaigns**
- **Embrace fluidity without understanding the impact on rights buying**

What's the challenge for marketers?

Of course media budgets dwarf those for production – If there's a chance to save £500K on a media opportunity which results in an additional £50K of music usage fees then perhaps that's a no brainer. Nevertheless, it's important to understand the consequences of a fluid media plan which doesn't match the third-party rights you've licensed. This affects not only music but also on-screen talent. The financial, legal and reputational consequences can be serious.

To find a workable solution, smart marketers should speak to both their media agency and an external music licensing expert.

Chapter summary

In this chapter we've learned that:

- **Alignment of music licence terms with required media usage is paramount**
- **Media schedules should be finalised up-front and not changed**
- **A fluid media schedule creates legal risk and licence fee inflation**
- **Media agencies should be encouraged to appreciate third-party IP risk**

Reader's notes

(i) Big Mental Note

(ii) One Big Step

SECTION FIVE
What's the role of creative agencies?

The decision to leave my previous business, a joint venture within a creative agency, and establish Resilient Music was triggered by various consulting projects performed in conjunction with marketing procurement consultancies. In most cases, I was brought in to "fire fight" a music licensing problem related to an external advertising agency, usually during production or post production. It was often too late to make a significant difference. The more projects I worked on, the more it became clear that the same patterns of behaviour were being repeated. These all appeared to be agency-driven practices though it's true that client indecision was often a significant factor. In this chapter, we'll look at some of these issues, examine the root problems and how they might be addressed.

CHAPTER 20
"Just in time" management

In this chapter we'll examine if the decision-making processes of some creative agencies can be an impediment to smart deal negotiation.

Having spent seven years inside a creative agency, it's clear that they tend to thrive on the adrenaline of urgency. Final creative decisions on music are often left to the last minute in a constant quest to find a better track or to prove that the agency's one recommendation is the right one. Whilst this might appear to be creatively admirable, it's commercially flawed as the agency sacrifices all negotiation power on behalf of its client.

Here are several extreme examples, drawn from real experiences:

(i) "I'll know it when I hear it"

Articulating a clear music brief is difficult – and not all agency creative teams have the language to do this. Some creatives might use obtuse phrases such as:

"I'll know it when I hear it"
"Don't rule anything out"

"Let's find something unexpected"

As a marketer, I suggest you should be deeply involved in the creative music brief and demand that the agency clearly articulates it in a manner that music rights owners will properly understand. If any of the above phrases arise in conversation during this process, alarm bells should ring. The outcome will be that lack of clarity leads to an eleventh hour decision and so a weak negotiating position.

(ii) "I can't hear if I can't see"

It's understandable that final music decisions need to be made in conjunction with the image – all concerned want to see the track laid to picture. However, that shouldn't mean there can be no discussion of music before post production. A reluctance to engage with music prior to production can delay decision-making and frequently leads to a poor commercial outcome.

(iii) "Not invented here"

Whilst not intrinsically about timing, the "not invented here" attitude is occasionally displayed by some agency creatives. A brilliant musical suggestion could come from an external supplier, account manager, producer, director, editors or even the client. However, if the creative team doesn't feel like they "own" that idea, sometimes they may be less willing to support it, even if it's right for the project.

Chapter summary

In this chapter we've learned that some creative agencies:

- **Delay final music decisions while striving to find the best track**
- **Delay final music decisions to justify their single track recommendation**
- **Fail to clearly articulate the music brief**
- **Resist properly considering music in the absence of a film**
- **Aren't fully open to creative music ideas from any source**

Reader's notes

(i) Big Mental Note

(ii) One Big Step

CHAPTER 21
Single track recommendation

In this chapter we'll examine why agencies make single track recommendations and how that impacts on licence fee negotiation.

We looked at this earlier but it's worth examining the issue further. Why is it that some creative agencies tend to make one music track recommendation to their clients claiming that no possible alternative could work?

(i) Sole arbiter of taste

Occasionally, there's an attitude within some creative agencies that "we know best" and hence the need to guide and cajole the client into accepting all creative recommendations. The thinking often goes that a client who willingly complies is brave whilst one who doesn't is blinkered.

This feeds into music recommendations from the presentation of the first mood film or animatic where often a wholly unaffordable track is used to convey the desired emotion. The more this track is heard, the more all concerned fall in love with it. In the film business it's called "temp love", where un-cleared music sits on a "temp track". In the advertising world, it's the same issue. I've seen instances where the agency waits until the client has truly fallen in love with a track before the rights owners are approached and fees discussed. Even when the sync licence fee quotes far exceed the allocated budget, the agency convinces the client to find more money to support the belief that no other possible music track could work. The agency positions itself as the sole arbiter of taste having convinced the client that it's brave to back their judgement. In these instances, commercial reason is set aside and the client is persuaded to pay far more for music than they originally intended.

(ii) One egg in one basket

Of course the above issue is the enemy of competition. As we've already discussed, where there's no back-up track, there's no "walk away" position. Music rights owners are highly tuned to detect that need and so increase sync licence fees.

Chapter summary

In this chapter we've learned that some creative agencies make single track recommendations to:

- **Enhance their role as sole arbiter of taste**
- **Suppress any creative dissent**

We've also learned that:

- **Single track recommendations weaken a brand's bargaining position**
- **Music rights owners are highly tuned to detect and exploit this**

Reader's notes

(i) Big Mental Note

(ii) One Big Step

CHAPTER 22
Nowhere to run

In this chapter we'll examine how the persuasive skills of agencies can be employed to restrict musical options for their clients. This often results in a poor commercial outcome.

(i) How to spot when you're being backed into a corner

Creative agencies are masters of persuasion. That's their *raison d'être* – to change consumers' attitudes and behaviours and choose their clients' brands rather than competitors. However, some less honourable agencies employ these skills to steer their clients towards an outcome which suits the agency's agenda.

In consulting projects my role is often as counsellor to beleaguered marketers who've come unstuck on a music deal. They frequently complain about being backed into a corner though don't always understand how this happened. After unpicking the story, a common pattern often emerges:

- **Single track recommended by agency during creative development**
- **Agency refuses to consider any alternative tracks**
- **Client falls in love with track**
- **Track remains on mood films, animatics, rough edits**
- **Negotiations with rights owners don't start until post production**
- **Rights owners' quotes significantly exceed available music budget**
- **Delivery date of film is fast approaching**
- **Media has already been booked and paid for**
- **Rights owners refuse to reduce quotes**
- **Approval process takes several days – "right up to the wire"**
- **Agency panics client into making a decision to buy the track**
- **Agency says: "Issue the PO now or we'll miss the media start date"**
- **Client concedes and spends far more than the allocated music budget**

I've seen this happen many times – The agency account director shrugs their shoulders in a "what can you do?" stance, when sometimes they have engineered this scenario to deliver the track the agency wanted all along. The client is left with no choice but to acquiesce, having no time and no back-up options.

Chapter summary

In this chapter we've learned that, as masters of persuasion, some agencies like to steer their clients to one musical solution when often others are worth considering. This removes the competitive element from negotiations with rights owners and often leads to a poor commercial outcome.

Reader's notes

(i) Big Mental Note

(ii) One Big Step

CHAPTER 23

Where's the return on investment?

For smart marketers to drive better value from music, we discussed the benefits of hero and back-up tracks in Section three, chapter 12. However, when comparing tracks of varying cost against one another, it's essential to consider their marketing effectiveness as well as cost efficiency. This is a question of Return On Investment ("ROI") which we'll explore in this chapter.

(i) How to demand accountability

If you've followed my advice so far and have insisted that music is considered before production begins, you'll hopefully have several tracks in consideration for your TV spot. You'll also have insisted that the rights owners have been approached, quotes have been secured and licence fees have been agreed. Inevitably some tracks will be more expensive than others and the agency will recommend their favourite.

Let's assume that in a shortlist of three tracks, you make a creative call that any one would work and are happy to take the cheapest or middle priced option. If the agency insists that only the most expensive track suits the campaign, make the agency financially accountable if the campaign doesn't deliver on agreed commercial outcome metrics. Such metrics may be increased brand awareness, sales revenue or other KPIs. This will encourage greater alignment with the brand's perspective that the cost of the production and campaign commercial outcomes are intrinsically linked.

Chapter summary

In this chapter we've learned that sometimes agencies

- **recommend tracks primarily on creative grounds**
- **consider cost to be a secondary issue**
- **fail to connect production cost with campaign commercial outcomes**

We've also explored how smart marketers can focus their agency's mind by

- **insisting that music is addressed before production**
- **multiple tracks are considered, checked and priced**
- **making the agency financially accountable for their recommendations**

Reader's notes

(i) Big Mental Note

(ii) One Big Step

CHAPTER 24
Commission-based brokering. Conflict of interest?

In this chapter we'll examine the fundamental flaw in how music rights are brokered by agencies' outsourced suppliers.

(i) The ten per-centers

Many UK creative agencies outsource music licence negotiations to external companies. There's a relatively small supply chain that serves the large London-based network agencies and many of these work on a commission basis. The suppliers are often referred to as sync agencies or clearance houses and their job, supposedly, is to broker the best deals for their client, the creative agency. There is however a fundamental flaw:

Their financial incentives work in the wrong direction because most suppliers charge 10% to 15% commission.

Let's stop to consider this. These suppliers are acting for the buyer, yet they're better rewarded when the seller makes more money. This is an obvious conflict of interest yet the practice continues to survive.

As a marketer you should demand transparency and full disclosure of the commercial terms between your agency and their supply chain. Any commission based model that works against your commercial interests should be fiercely challenged.

(ii) The insanity of the status quo

Given the manner in which client-side marketing procurement teams have challenged agency fees, it's surprising that they haven't yet tackled the supplier commission model I've described above. Until procurement teams do this, it will never change. The agencies won't challenge it as it's not their money that's being spent. The more production costs are reduced, the more exposed are their agency fees. So the agencies have a vested interest in the status quo.

Chapter summary

In this chapter we've learned that:

- **Many agencies outsource music licensing tasks to external suppliers**
- **Suppliers are known as "sync agencies" & "clearance houses"**
- **Many suppliers charge commission on sync fees paid to rights owners**
- **Commission rates are 10% – 15%**
- **Agencies are unlikely to challenge this model**

Reader's notes

(i) Big Mental Note

(ii) One Big Step

CHAPTER 25

Apparently independent? The hidden owned and affiliated music companies

In this chapter we'll look at the status of music search and clearance suppliers to whom many creative agencies outsource music sourcing and licensing tasks.

(i) The danger of preferred suppliers

Most companies have preferred suppliers, both brands and agencies alike. That's perfectly fine provided that one can justify the added value in comparison to competitors. As client-side procurement teams have challenged agency fees, agencies have sought to make up the shortfall elsewhere. It's no longer possible to justify mark-ups on supply chain fees, so some agencies have established their own specialist divisions to extract financial rewards by another route, rather than outsource to external suppliers. For those that don't want set up new ventures, they acquire or partner with third party specialist suppliers. This is an established trend with post-production and more recently content production, where many agency groups now have their own facilities. It has also happened in music.

As a marketer, you should demand transparency concerning the suppliers who find and buy music tracks for your agency, specifically for your account. Check if these suppliers:

- **Are owned or part owned by the agency**
- **Are owned or part owned by the marketing services group that owns the agency**
- **Have an exclusive arrangement with the agency**
- **Have their staff inside the agency**

If any of the above apply, it's likely that the agency / supplier relationship isn't truly independent and competitive – hence your brand may not be getting the best deal on music-related fees.

(ii) How to demand a level playing field

Where you find that your agency's relationship with their preferred music supplier isn't independent, demand that the agency puts the task out to tender so you can compare commercial terms and fees against at least two other proven independent suppliers. If this is met with fierce resistance from your agency, this may be proof that the agency has a vested financial interest in working solely with the preferred supplier.

Chapter summary

In this chapter we've learned that:

- **Agency fees are under pressure**
- **Agencies look to make up the shortfall through other means**
- **Some agencies establish specialist music operations rather than outsource**
- **Others acquire or exclusively partner with external suppliers**
- **These arrangements may be geared to drive agency profitability**

We've also learned that smart marketers should

- **Challenge their agency's supply chain**
- **Examine any exclusive or equity-based relationships**
- **Mandate that suppliers are sourced through competitive tendering**

Reader's notes

(i) Big Mental Note

(ii) One Big Step

SECTION SIX

Five practical steps to implement before planning your next campaign

By reading this book, you'll have learned about the common problems which impact marketers when sourcing and buying music for their campaigns. More importantly, you now have an understanding of how to avoid them in future. To help you drive change and secure buy-in from your colleagues and agencies, I've set out a simple five-step plan to implement on your next campaign.

CHAPTER 26
Starting earlier

You'll have "heard it all before" from colleagues and other suppliers, but here's why starting earlier with music matters.

(i) Pre-research

Whether you're testing one or several scripts before green-lighting production, it's likely that you'll want to create an animatic which often contains an agency-recommended music track. Frequently, both the marketing team and their agency fall in love with this track, which becomes deeply embedded in the creative concept.

Mistake

Most brands ask their agency to dub music to the animatic that will be tested in Research. However, agencies frequently fail to check up-front whether the music track is clearable and at what cost.

Solution

- **Make sure you have multiple track options, laid back to picture, to be tested in Research**
- **Map qualitative output of Research against music cost for an informed decision**

(ii) Pre-production

Whether or not the tracks tested at Research stage stay attached to the project, I'd still recommend music be on the agenda during Pre-Production.

Mistake

Most brands allow their agency to delay dealing with music until the film is in post-production with very little time to find and license tracks.

Solution

- **Mandate that music search & licensing tasks are built into pre-production schedule**
- **Use competitive tendering for sourcing music (see Section Three, Chapter 12)**

CHAPTER 27
Media schedules

(i) Centralised buying

For global marketing executives who deal with music, unlicensed usage and weak bargaining positions are a real headache. This happens when rights are bought centrally but local markets neither notify their requirements in advance nor comply with licence restrictions. This can lead to claims against the global marketing team and/or their agency.

Mistake

Many global marketing teams don't have sufficient control or visibility over their local markets' media buying. This creates significant risk when third-party IP rights are bought centrally to be used locally. This risk applies to music, on-screen talent, bespoke photography, "stock library" assets and any other third-party IP.

Solution

- **Set advance deadlines for local markets to advise media requirements**
- **Deadlines must be set-in-stone before pre-production**

- Insist on total compliance
- Build local media requirements into usage rights bought for all third-party IP
- Reduce risk of unlicensed usage, especially in autonomous local markets

(ii) Local market accountability

Mistake

Many global marketing teams attempt to implement the above process but still absorb the additional costs when local market non-compliance results in unlicensed usage.

Solution

- Follow process in (i) Centralised Buying above
- Insist on complete compliance from all local markets
- Make local markets financially responsible for any additional usage costs arising from non-compliance

CHAPTER 28
Competitive tendering

Economicshelp.org defines competitive tendering as:
"When firms bid for the right to run a service or gain a
certain contract"

Your company already uses competitive tendering to purchase most goods and services. Indeed, the selection of your creative and media agencies probably went through a commercially robust pitch process, often managed by an independent trade body or intermediary.

In contrast, it's likely that music is currently sourced and purchased for your campaigns without any similar commercial discipline. The process is therefore creatively-led. You, or your agency, find a track that you like and pay what it costs, with perhaps some minor negotiation. The balance of power in this transaction sits with the supplier. This can be changed with competitive tendering.

(i) Creative and commercial briefs

Mistake

Most brands allow their agencies to issue music briefs that focus solely on creative requirements. This adheres to the industry mantra of "not restricting creativity" but fails to recognise the commercial realities of rights and budget.

Solution

- **Have the creative agency define what you want your audience to feel**
- **Build your creative brief around that**
- **Use the media agency's plan to define usage requirements for third-party IP**
- **Clarify the music allocation within the production budget**
- **Build the commercial brief around required media & available budget**

(ii) Implementation

Mistake

Most brands allow their creative agency to subcontract music sourcing to external suppliers with little visibility on the music rights owners those suppliers approach to find music tracks. There's a risk that only favourite rights owners are approached where vested interests are at play.

Solution

- Work directly with an independent supplier who grants full visibility on the sourcing process

(iii) Watch-outs

Mistake

Your creative agency will resist competitive tendering for sourcing music. They'll complain it will restrict creativity. Many brands back down from this confrontation.

Solution

- Embrace competitive tendering as a form of filtering
- It's designed to remove tracks that are neither affordable nor available
- Insist that your agency buys into this responsible process
- Make the agency accountable for any compliance breach

CHAPTER 29
Future proofing

As we learned in Section 3, Chapter 13, licence options are your defence against uncontrollable fee escalation for on-going usage. If deployed correctly, they allow you to future-proof your music deals. Success relies on careful planning before you start the first licence negotiations. Get it wrong, and the music rights owners will show no mercy in hiking up fees where they feel the balance of power rests on their side.

(i) Holistic view across full agency roster

Mistake

Many brands treat their creative agency as the "lead", allowing them to buy third-party IP rights for the assets they create – of course this includes music. However, the creative agency has no real incentive to establish how the client's other roster agencies might use those assets or indeed create new ones featuring the same music. Time and again, none or insufficient options are included in the first licence to cover all the possible uses of the music that the brand may need, irrespective of which roster agency creates the asset, whether that's the creative, digital, PR, social or even media agency.

Solution

- **The brand, not the creative agency, should contract with music rights owners**
- **This gives the brand greater control, irrespective of who created the asset**
- **Share creative agency's concept, including music, with whole agency roster**
- **Do this very early during the campaign's development**
- **Mandate that all roster agencies suggest how the music will be used**
- **Seek expert help to collate the usage and negotiate the rights**

(ii) Multiple content

Mistake

It's not just the usage, it's the multiple content pieces within an overarching campaign that must be defined if you intend that these pieces use the same music. Many brands fail to properly collate this information – what music rights owners call "context" – essentially what viewers will see when the music is heard.

Solution

Following on from section (i) above, mandate that all your agencies clearly articulate:

- **The visual content of each film or online activation**
- **The manner in which the music will be used**
- **The strategy that links the various content pieces**

(iii) Past, present, future

Mistake

When I offer the advice set out in (i) and (ii) above to brands, the common response is "we just don't know yet". This stance might feel like a plausible excuse, but it's really an abdication of responsibility. By not capturing the intended music usage from the outset, your company will be exposed to uncontrollable music licence fee inflation. In this context, the music rights owners will have strong bargaining power whilst your negotiating position will be weak.

Solution

If you "just don't know yet", then you can still make some educated guesses about proposed future usage and cover that as Options into your licence. Remember – options cost you nothing until you exercise them. So, if it turns out you've negotiated an option you don't need, don't exercise it. However it's far better to have options in the licence as a means to control future fee inflation.

CHAPTER 30
Compliance

(i) Monitoring

Mistake

It's no good following all of the above advice if you still can't monitor compliance across your local markets and agencies. Human nature dictates that most people only follow the rules when there are direct personal consequences for breaking them. Some global marketing teams may wish to avoid possible argument with their agencies and local market colleagues. This approach may lead to "rogue" behaviour and therefore unlicensed music usage.

Solution

- **Make local markets and their agencies accountable**
- **Carry out random post-campaign audits using independent experts**

(ii) Upskilling

Mistake

Many brand marketers take insufficient interest in the buying of third-party IP rights. When questioned on this, the common response is "Our agency takes care of that, so I don't need to worry about it". Again, this is an abdication of responsibility because whilst the agency might be tasked with IP rights buying, they generally don't suffer the legal and financial consequences of getting it wrong – it's typically the brand that picks up the tab.

Solution

- Train your marketing team in the basics of music rights
- It doesn't need to be overtly legal training, but it must be practical
- Train your agencies in the same way
- Ensure that marketing and agency teams "buy in" to the programme
- Use independent proven experts to deliver the training

YOUR NEXT STEPS TO LICENSING SUCCESS

Having read this book, you should now have a better understanding of:

- **How the music industry is structured**
- **How music rights work and which ones you need to license**
- **What drives the cost of music and how to manage it**
- **What risks exist and how to manage them**
- **What role do creative agencies play**

I'm well aware there's a lot to take in here and you may still feel confused in some areas. I regularly work with clients who want to improve their understanding of music rights across their marketing teams and agencies in order to drive better commercial outcomes.

I frequently run training sessions and workshops for brand teams, marketing procurement executives and even in-house counsel on music rights. To find out more, get in touch with me at:

Email richard@resilientmusic.com

Tel +44 (0) 20 3137 0324

If you'd like to connect on LinkedIn, I have an active Music Procurement Group in which we debate music licensing issued. Connect with me at: uk.linkedin.com/in/richardkirstein

I regularly publish blog posts and eBooks which provide further useful information and discuss topical points on music licensing.

For our latest blog posts, go to: http://resilientmusic.com/music-procurement-blog/

For our eBooks, such as The A To Z Of Music Licensing, get in touch at:

Email richard@resilientmusic.com

You can also contact me via Twitter or our website

Twitter @resilientmusic
Web resilientmusic.com

GLOSSARY OF TERMS

Advance – A sum of money advanced against future royalties paid by music publishers to songwriters and/or by record labels to recording artists usually in return for entering into an exclusive agreement for a given period of time.

AFofM – American Federation of Musicians. The USA-based trades union representing the interests of non-featured session musicians.

Approval Chain – The multiple parties whose consent is required in order for a rights owner to grant a synchronisation licence to a licensee e.g. a brand or advertising agency.

Approval Party – The individual party whose consent is required in order for a rights owner to grant a synchronisation licence to a licensee e.g. a brand or advertising agency.

Arranger – An accomplished musician able to take an existing song or composition and create instrumental and/or vocal parts usually to be performed by session musicians and/or backing singers for a recording session or live performance. For example, an arranger might create string parts (violin, viola, cello and double bass) or horn parts (e.g. trumpet, trombone, saxophone).

Artist Manager – Represents featured artists, almost always on an exclusive basis, across all or most elements of their career.

ATL – Short for "Above The Line". Usually applies to Television, Radio and Cinema bought advertising media.

B2B – Business to business

B2C – Business to consumer

Bespoke Music – Also known as "commissioned music" or "score". It's music that's written to order by a composer, to a brief from a brand or advertising agency.

Blanket Licence – A licence that covers multiple songs or sound recordings, usually granted by a Performing Right Organisation (e.g. PRS or PPL) and not requiring individual prior consent per song or sound recording.

Booking Agent – Represents featured artists, usually on an exclusive basis, solely in their capacity as live performers.

BPI – British Phonographic Institute. The UK trade body representing major record labels.

Breach of Licence – Use of a copyright song, composition or sound recording beyond the agreed terms of an existing licence.

Buy-out – A confusing term frequently used to mean licence.

CD – Compact Disc (rather than Creative Director)

Commercial Catalogue – Also known as "needle drop" in the USA. It usually means music created by songwriters and recorded by recording artists for commercial release to the general public.

Commission based brokering – The practice of synchronisation clearance companies, acting for brands or advertising agencies as licensees, charging a commission mark-up on the licence fees they negotiate with rights owner licensors.

Competitive tendering – Defined by economicshelp.org as "when firms bid for the right to run a service or gain a certain contract".

Conductor – The person who directs a musical ensemble such as an orchestra or choir. The conductor usually stands at the front of the ensemble waving a baton to mark the rhythmic beats of the musical bar. In a live performance context, the conductor usually has their back to the audience.

Context – Usually means the visual context in which the licensed music will be used (i.e. what the viewers see when the music is heard within a commercial or online video).

Co-publishers – One song or composition can be jointly owned by two or more music publishers. These joint owners are usually called co-publishers (or "co-pubs").

Copyright Infringement – Use of a copyright song, composition or sound recording without a valid licence in place.

Cover Artist – A recording artist who records their own new version of a song or composition previously recorded and/or made famous by an earlier recording artist.

Creative agency – Usually an advertising agency with the remit to develop both brand strategy and creative concepts for their advertiser clients and usually implement those concepts through production of finished content e.g. TV commercials or online videos.

Digital Audio File – A computer file containing a captured audio signal. Professional formats include .wav and .aiff whereas most domestic uses involve .mp3 or similar.

Estate – Usually surviving spouse or family members who control the interests of a deceased songwriter, composer or artist.

Exclusivity – In the context of synchronisation licensing – a licence provision that prevents the rights owners from granting a simultaneous licence to other brands in a single or multiple product category.

Featured Artist – The named recording artist attributed to a commercially released sound recording, usually the singer and/or the permanent members of an ensemble under an exclusive recording agreement with a record label.

Fixer – The person who sources (and represents) non-featured artists e.g. session musicians and backing singers, usually on a non-exclusive basis, for recording sessions and live performances.

Geo locking – Also known as Geo blocking. The ability to restrict the availability of online content, usually videos, to specific territories or markets. Geo locking is, at the time of writing, available on YouTube partner channels.

Indie – Short for Independent. Any music rights owner company that isn't a Major.

Industrial – Catch-all term for any licensed media which isn't ATL or Online e.g. conferences, trade shows, exhibitions, events, internal.

IP – Intellectual Property – an intangible asset

Licensee – The party that has to negotiate and agree terms with the licensor in order to receive the benefit of the licence granted by the licensor. This is effectively the buyer as the licensee would usually pay a licence fee for the privilege of receiving the licence.

Licensor – The party that owns, controls or administers music copyright and can grant a licence for its usage. This is the effectively the seller as the licensor would usually expect to receive a licence fee for the privilege of granting the licence.

Lyrics – Words written by a lyricist usually to be sung to a melody. Also known as libretto within operatic works.

Major – The term currently applied to the three largest corporate music rights owner groups namely Universal, Warner (including Warner Chappell) and Sony (including SonyATV).

Master Rights – The copyright in a sound recording, usually controlled by a record label.

MCPS – Short for Mechanical Copyright Protection Society. MCPS is part of PRS for Music and licenses the mechanical right in the UK for songs and compositions on behalf of music publishers (for published works) and unpublished songwriters and composers.

Mechanical licence – A licence granted by the owner of a song or composition (or their appointed collection society e.g. MCPS) to allow the mechanical reproduction on vinyl, CD or digital download, usually for commercial sale.

Media – Or "Licensed Media" – The specific media or channels that the sync licence covers e.g. All Media, Broadcast TV, Cinema, Radio, Online.

Media agency – An agency with the remit to advise on media channel strategy for their advertiser clients and then implement that strategy through media buying.

Media Schedule – A detailed plan, usually created in Excel, showing blocks of days or weeks for bought media usage.

MFN – Most Favoured Nations. An upwards only price equalisation device imposed by music rights owners within synchronisation licences that ensures the value of song and sound recording are equal within the same campaign usage.

MU – Short for Musicians Union. The UK trades union representing the interests of non-featured session musicians or backing singers.

Music publisher – A company that owns or administers songs, compositions or lyrics on behalf of songwriters, composers and lyricists.

Musical work – A song with lyrics created by a songwriter or instrumental composition created by a composer

Musicologist – An expert in both musical analysis and copyright infringement legal practice in respect of sound-a-like and passing off claims.

Non-featured Artist – Session musicians and backing singers engaged to perform on a sound recording but who aren't permanent members of the featured artist ensemble nor are subject to an exclusive recording agreement with the featured artist's record label.

Option – A provision within a synchronisation licence to fix the licence fee of a specific future usage, defined by Term, Territory, Media or Context of Use. Options nearly always must be exercised prior to the expiry of an existing Term or a specified deadline.

Option Fee – The licence fee paid by the licensee to the licensor for the privilege of exercising a licence Option.

Out Of Copyright – The state of works that are no longer in copyright term

Passing off – A re-record of an existing song or composition that's intentionally similar to another existing sound recording.

Performers union – A trades union that represents non-featured artists such as session musicians or backing singers. In the UK, these are Musicians Union and Equity respectively.

Performing Right – Also known as "public performance right". It's the right to "publicly perform" a song or sound recording by way of online transmission, broadcast, use within commercial premises or within a live performance.

PPL – Phonographic Performance Ltd. The UK's Performing Right Organisation ("PRO") that licenses the public performing right in sound recordings on behalf of performers and record labels.

Production Library Music – Also known as "mood music" or "stock music". It's the musical equivalent of library stock images

PRS for Music – Performing Right Society. The UK's Performing Right Organisation ("PRO") that licenses the public performing right in songs and compositions on behalf of songwriters, lyricists, composers and music publishers.

Public Domain – The state of works that are no longer in copyright term or were never protected by copyright law.

Publishing Rights – The copyright in a song, lyrics or composition, usually controlled by a music publisher.

Record label – A company that owns or has a license to commercially release sound recordings featuring the performances of featured and/or non-featured artists

Record Producer – Also known as a producer. A creative individual who may also be a musician, songwriter and/or recording engineer. The record producer's role is to secure the best possible performance of a recording artist within a recording studio context and deliver the best possible finished recording to the artist and their record label. This broad remit can include re-structuring and re-arrangement of a song, the choice of arrangers, session musicians and backing singers.

Recording Artist – A musical performer who records their performance of a song or composition

Re-mix – The creation of a new audio balance between the individual vocal and instrumental parts of a "multi-track" sound recording. This requires access to the digital audio file "stems" which may have been copied from the original analogue multi-track tape for pre 1990s sound recordings.

Re-record – Within the advertising industry this usually means a newly commissioned sound recording of an existing song or composition, specifically created for use within a marketing campaign.

Rights Owner – In the context of music, it usually means the party that controls the copyright in a song, sound recording, image, name, likeness or other right.

Session musicians – Freelance musicians who are engaged on a project basis for recording sessions or live performances.

Song – A musical composition usually with lyrics created by a songwriter

Songwriter – The creator of the music and/or lyrics of a song

Sound recording – The audio capture of the performance of a song or composition, whether within a recording studio or live performance context

Sound-a-like – A supposedly new composition that's intentionally similar to another existing work.

Spot Times – An itemised commercial spot-by-spot analysis, usually of bought broadcast media such as TV, detailing the precise time, date, channel, market and editorial programme within which each spot was broadcast.

Synchronisation – Also known as Sync or Synch. The act of fixing music against moving images within audio-visual media.

Synchronisation licence – A contract issued by the rights owners of songs / compositions and/or sound recordings which grants permission for synchronisation to take place.

Synchronisation licence fee – The fee payable to the rights owners of songs / compositions and/or sound recordings for the privilege of granting a synchronisation licence.

Tempo – Musical speed usually measured in beats per minute ("BPM").

Term – Or "Licensed Term" – The duration of a licence (e.g. three, six or twelve months).

Territory – Or "Licensed Territory" – The countries or markets that the licence covers e.g. Worldwide, Europe, UK .

Three Strikes Rule – The procedure adopted by YouTube whereby after three instances of video takedown due to unlicensed music usage, the entire YouTube channel is suspended.

Track – Usually means sound recording rather than song.

Unpublished song – A song that hasn't been assigned or licensed to a music publisher by its songwriter(s). Also known as being in a "copyright control" state.

Unpublished songwriter – A songwriter that isn't subject to an exclusive song writing agreement with a music publisher.

Unsigned artist – A recording artist that isn't subject to an exclusive recording agreement with a record label.

Writer Splits – One song or composition can be jointly written by two or more songwriters or composers. The equity share isn't necessarily proportional but has to be agreed between the parties. This final division of the song is called the writer splits.

ACKNOWLEDGEMENTS

My special thanks to following people who generously gave their time to read the early drafts and provide insightful feedback: Stacey Hope, Amy Modell, Susan Stone, Rob Hoile, Jeff Cobb and Natalie O'Neill.

Thank you for Dominic Chambers, Paul Hibbs and Billy Burgess for their kind words of support.

Thank you to Steve Lightfoot and Traci Dunne for their generous support and encouragement in my quest to educate marketers in music licensing.

Thank you to Frances Royle and Michael Hardman for their belief and support at pivotal moments in my music licensing career.

Thank you to Kevin Duncan for his encouragement and practical advice.

Thank you to Emma Thompson for diligent assistance.

Thank you to Jane Woodyer, Joanne McGowan and Adam Webb for expert online promotion and PR support.

Thank you to Lucy McCarraher and Joe Gregory for their publishing and editorial support.

THE AUTHOR

Richard Kirstein is the UK's leading independent expert on music rights buying for brands. During a career spanning over twenty years, he has brokered several thousand music licences, acting for both rights buyers and sellers. He is a regular speaker at conferences in the UK, Europe and USA.

Since 2010, Richard has been Founding Partner of Resilient Music LLP, a successful specialist consultancy with team members in London and New York. Resilient's clients include some of the world's largest consumer brands in thefashion, automotive, financial services and alcoholic beverage sectors.

Prior to Resilient, Richard was Managing Director of Leap Music, a joint venture he established with advertising agency Bartle Bogle Hegarty (BBH). Leap was the first music publishing company inside a UK creative agency, upsetting many in the music industry by empowering brands to acquire copyright in bespoke commissioned scores. During Richard's tenure, Leap also negotiated over one thousand sync licences for music in TV spots.

Before Leap, Richard was Head of Film, TV & Media at Zomba Music Publishers. Richard established Zomba's UK sync licensing team, brokering deals for songs recorded by artists ranging from Bruce Springsteen to Daft Punk. He also brokered publishing administration deals with TV broadcasters and production companies including Channel 4 and Aardman Animations.

Richard is a music graduate from The City University, London and Guildhall School of Music and Drama. He continued his education at Dartington College of Arts and London Business School. Outside Resilient Richard attends many gigs, composes music for several UK production music libraries and occasionally plays keyboards in cover bands. He lives outside London and has two teenage sons, both musicians.

Lightning Source UK Ltd.
Milton Keynes UK
UKOW07f2044271115

263653UK00003B/132/P